A PASSION FOR *Prayer*

We read in Acts 6 that the apostles gave themselves to prayer and the ministry of the Word. Truly, Vonette Bright followed their lead and, in so doing, became an example to many of us. Her example, prayers and exhortations have had an impact on me. What an example as a wife—not only a helpmeet, but also as an encourager of women and a leader; a woman of grace and courage; a woman who, because of her intimate relationship with God, demonstrated her faith and the power of prayer in the home-going of her beloved Bill.

Kay Arthur
Co-CEO, Precept Ministries International

I am still humbled by Vonette's faithful reliance on God through daily conversations with Him. Her influence in prayer has gone beyond the United States to the world through her prayer workshops, the International Prayer Assembly and the Lausanne Committee.

Ev Davis
The *JESUS* Film Project

Vonette's passion and perseverance in mobilizing others to pray have been extraordinary—she has pressed on in the battle when most would have wearied and moved on to less demanding and daunting tasks. As a widow in her 80s, no one would have faulted her for wanting to relax a bit and leave the heavy lifting of prayer to younger backs. But like Anna, that indefatigable, elderly widow of old, Vonette has not departed from His presence, "worshiping with fasting and prayer night and day" (Luke 2:37, *ESV*), giving thanks to God for the fulfillment of His promises in Christ, and speaking of Him to all who are waiting and longing for His redemption.

Nancy Leigh DeMoss
Author and Host of *Revive Our Hearts* radio

Vonette Bright is one of the nation's true prayer warriors. In 1998, she led the successful effort in Congress to designate the first Thursday in May as the National Day of Prayer, and now she has written this important book on the subject of prayer. Vonette is one of the great ladies of the Christian Church, and I thank God for her courage and conviction.

Shirley Dobson
Chairman of the National Day of Prayer Task Force

Vonette's life of prayer has greatly influenced my passion for prayer for the world, starting from my Judea, Samaria and to the uttermost parts of the earth. Her modeling of prayer, teaching people how to pray, and mobilizing the Body of Christ to pray for revival and spiritual awakening in America is something that I will emulate for the rest of my life!

Aida Laureta Force
Inner City Staff, Here's Life

When I think of Vonette Bright, I think of an active Christian life that is rooted in regular conversation with Jesus Christ. Her freedom of dialogue prayer has inspired hope and joy.

Tim Goeglein
Vice President for External Relations, Focus on the Family

One of the great experiences of my life has been to know Vonette and Bill Bright for more than 60 years. From our first meeting in 1949 in the home of Henrietta Mears, I have seen in both a heart for the gospel and an extraordinary vision to reach people for Jesus Christ. Vonette has always built her life and ministry on the Scriptures and prayer. Her single-minded focus on the power of intercessory prayer has been both an encouragement to my own life and a model for the Church. Heavenly records will one day reveal the full impact of her prayer life and teaching ministry in the lives of countless persons who have come to faith in Christ.

Billy Graham
Evangelist and Author

Vonette has been a dear friend, a wonderful mentor and a loving shepherd. She has nurtured my faith in every imaginable way and has taught me again and again that God can do anything. Her message has not just been for me but also for every man and woman. No one has served me more kindly or more profoundly than Vonette Bright.

Mary Graham
Women of Faith

Because of Vonette Bright's dedication to prayer, my husband and I have also become "prayer warriors." Thank you, Vonette, for your example as a Christian to all who know you!

Sharon and Marvin Joyner
The *JESUS* Film Project

Listening to Vonette talk about prayer is like drinking a Diet Coke . . . it makes me so hungry. Vonette always makes me hungry for more prayer.

Josh McDowell
Author and Speaker

Vonette's passion for the Word and applying it and her passion for prayer has changed my life. Thank you, Vonette, for your life and example of a *woman of God for all of us!*

Jeannie McKean
Associate Director, M-Track, Campus Crusade for Christ

I have so appreciated and highly respected Vonette's daily walk and trust in the Lord. I am so humbled by her sweet spirit and godly desire to be so dependent on the Lord in all things. She has laid the wonderful foundation of prayer for this movement.

Milt Monell
Director, Great Commission Global Prayer Movement

I can't think of a single person on the planet that I respect more than Vonette Bright. She is 10 feet tall in my eyes. Like so many others, I have been profoundly impacted by her long obedience. She is a gift to our generation.

Beth Moore
Living Proof Ministries

Vonette Bright has been the single biggest influence in my life for making prayer a priority for our nation, our ministry and for me personally. Her faithful leadership has called millions globally to worship God, bring their thanksgiving to Him, confess their sins, and petition the King of king and Lord of lords. I thank God for her model of persevering prayer.

Dr. Dennis Rainey
President and CEO, FamilyLife

Vonette has encouraged me to be a woman of prayer and a woman of indefatigable witness for Christ to those around her. She travels and encourages Christians to fulfill their purpose to "become blameless and pure, children of God without fault in a warped and crooked generation, [shining] like stars in the universe" (Phil. 2:15, *NIV*).

Dawn Sundstrom
Area Regional Director for Austria, Germany and Switzerland, Community Bible Study International

Vonette has been a role model for me in so many ways, but in particular in her commitment and passion for prayer! As I grew in my leadership, the Lord used Vonette's example to help me emphasize prayer throughout our ministry. Her influence is seen throughout the nation and the world. Personally, I have watched her champion prayer and empower others to be involved with her.

Nancy Wilson
Global Ambassador for CCC/Spokesperson for StoryRunners

We love Vonette as a sister in Christ, we love her for her joyful countenance, we love her for her godly wisdom, we love her for her passion for prayer and the kingdom of God, and we love her for continuing the heritage of support and encouragement that we consistently saw in her beloved Bill.

Frank Wright, Ph.D.
President and CEO, National Religious Broadcasters

I remember coming home from Campus Crusade staff training in the 1970s and buying a new prayer journal after I heard Mrs. Bright speak on prayer. She gave me the motivation and suggestions I needed to make specific prayer a reality in my life. Her encouragement and example spoke truth into my life, and still does.

Genie Zook
Internship Coordinator, Global Aid Network

What Happens When
You Speak and God Listens

A Passion for Prayer

VONETTE BRIGHT

Regal

For more information and
special offers from Regal Books, email us at
subscribe@regalbooks.com

Published by Regal
From Gospel Light
Ventura, California, U.S.A.
www.regalbooks.com
Printed in the U.S.A.

Library of Congress Cataloging-in-Publication Data
Bright, Vonette Z.
A passion for prayer : what happens when you speak and God listens /
Vonette Bright.
p. cm.
Includes bibliographical references.
ISBN 978-0-8307-5747-3 (hard cover)
1. Prayer—Christianity. I. Title.
BV210.3.B7375 2012
248.3'2—dc23
2011042587

Rights for publishing this book outside the U.S.A. or in non-English languages are
administered by Gospel Light Worldwide, an international not-for-profit ministry.
For additional information, please visit www.glww.org, email info@glww.org, or write
to Gospel Light Worldwide, 1957 Eastman Avenue, Ventura, CA 93003, U.S.A.

To order copies of this book and other Regal products in bulk quantities,
please contact us at 1-800-446-7735.

O Lord, hear me as I pray;
pay attention to my groaning.
Listen to my cry for help, my King and my God,
for I will never pray to anyone but you.
Listen to my voice in the morning, Lord.
Each morning I bring my requests to you
and wait expectantly.

PSALM 5:1-3

DEDICATION

The National Prayer Committee
Great Commission Prayer Crusade
The Great Commission Global Prayer Movement

CONTENTS

ACKNOWLEDGMENTS

When Bill and I were married, he was directing a deputation group that met on Friday evenings and divided into groups to go to jails, rescue missions, hospitals and, sometimes, churches. Although I felt comfortable to pray formally, this group talked to God as though He were in the room. This was totally foreign to me. I had to spend time working on my prayers, while they prayed so casually.

I soon learned that they prayed expectantly, thanking and praising God, and that they requested specifically what they desired God to do. When they returned each week, they were excited to share the answers to their prayers. Needless to say, I was growing in my faith by leaps and bounds.

Dr. Henrietta Mears led me to Christ, and I learned from her to pray specifically—naming exactly what I desired from God. One evening at Forest Home Conference Center, Dr. Mears led a service around a bonfire in which she requested each of us to lay a stick of wood on the fire as a symbol of a request of something we wanted God to do in our lives. I decided to ask God to "make me a woman of prayer." I forgot about that request until years later when God directly led me to a ministry of prayer.

As you can see, acknowledging those dear ones who influenced my life of prayer is a humbling process.

I am so grateful to the folks at Regal for allowing me to capture the practical lessons I have learned about prayer, and I pray that this book will inspire many to find new excitement about seeking God.

Chapter I

My Passion for Prayer

Prayer is the greatest privilege and most revolutionary power available to the Christian, and God's Word promises us its effectiveness.

Although you can get almost any information, on any subject, at the click of your computer keys, never before in the history of man have there been so many questions with so few answers. That's because most of the challenges we face are not the kind for which you simply consult a search engine. Most of our world's challenges need spiritual answers that must come through spiritual people. And spiritual people are people of prayer.

The Early Church demonstrated the power of united prayer as believers came together and prayed with one heart, mind and spirit. We, too, must become a people of extraordinary prayer, calling Christians of all denominations to pray for a moral and spiritual awakening throughout the world.

You and I have the privilege of calling on God in united, specific prayer to have a part in changing the world, our personal lives and our circumstances. We have God's promise that if we, who know Him personally, are willing to humble ourselves before Him, pray and turn from sin, He will bring the healing influence of His Spirit into our society (see 2 Chron. 7:14).

But first we must be individuals who pray. It is difficult to believe God for national and worldwide needs until we have seen

Him provide for our own personal needs. Faith, like a muscle of the body, needs exercise to grow. Since prayer is one way of expressing our faith, in order for prayer to be effective, our faith must increase as well. Once we have begun to see answers to our personal prayers, it is much easier to believe God for answers to prayers concerning our country and the rest of the world.

I celebrated a milestone birthday while working on this book. And I recognized with a grateful heart how many years a passion for prayer has been part of my life. I know beyond a doubt that God moved upon my heart with the realization that through united, specific, strategic and earnest prayer, we can move the hand of God and have a part in helping change the world. That is such a powerful thought, and I have seen it work!

My dear husband, Bill, knew the power of prayer, and he stated it so well:

> History records no significant movement of the Spirit of God that has not been preceded by a very strong prayer emphasis. And rightly so, because the omnipotent God has chosen to communicate with individuals through prayer, and through His inspired Word.
>
> Our Savior—to whom all authority in heaven and earth was given—spent much time praying while here on earth. Now seated at the right hand of God the Father in the place of authority in heaven, He has given Himself to prayer on our behalf. Since He is our example, we can rightly conclude that prayer is the highest calling that a Christian can have.
>
> A vast reservoir of power, wisdom and grace becomes available to us through prayer. All we must do is be willing to trust and obey the One to whom we pray.

Vonette Bright · www.regalbooks.com

As James states, "The reason you don't have what you want is that you don't ask God for it" (Jas. 4:2). Likewise, Jesus states, "If you believe, you will receive whatever you ask for in prayer" (Matt. 21:22).

The example of our Lord in prayer and the promises of God have encouraged millions of believers to enter into this great adventure of prayer. My husband knew the incredible power of prayer and truly experienced the reality of praying "without ceasing."

It is my heart's desire that every believer discover the enabling power of the Holy Spirit to become more personally involved in praying for a supernatural outpouring of God's Spirit for a worldwide revival. To that purpose, in addition to reading this book, there are many other excellent books available to you that are focused on prayer. I encourage you to read as many of these books as possible and practice the principles they teach.

Throughout the years of my ministry, I have participated in the development of materials used by our Campus Crusade staff as well as by many individuals around the world. It is my goal to present content that will motivate and equip you to develop a personal prayer ministry and get you excited about extending your prayer influence to your family, church and community.

This book is designed to enhance your communion with your heavenly Father. Used with your favorite Bible translation, it will enrich your times of worship, prayer and intercession by providing you with an orderly method of recording your requests, impressions and concerns for yourself, your family, your friends and the world around you.

I hope you will write in its pages and keep it as a permanent and chronological record of God's faithfulness as you note your spiritual growth and answers to your prayers. I promise this will increase your faith in God's limitless love, power and resources. Prayer has played a significant role in my life. God became a reality to me as I learned to pray and experienced answers to prayer.

Just a little history on my prayer passion . . .

When I became a Christian after graduating from college, and just before my husband and I were married, I met a group of people who prayed fervently and saw answers to their prayers. My husband was directing a deputation group that went to jails, road camps, hospitals and churches to share their faith in Jesus. We met together for prayer and team assignments on Friday evening. I did much of my spiritual growing as a result of those meetings, and it was great preparation for the beginning of Campus Crusade for Christ. Our first act was to mobilize a 24-hour prayer chain by dividing the 24 hours in a day into 96 15-minute segments. Prayer has continued to be a major emphasis of the Campus Crusade movement ever since.

In December 1971, God called me to a special emphasis on prayer as a result of a number of events. The Feminist Movement, spawned by angry, disillusioned, frustrated women activists in the 1950s caused me great concern for the effect it would have on the family. True, there were inequities of opportunity and salary for women that needed to be corrected; but to accomplish that by angry demonstrations and demands seemed so demeaning and unfeminine.

The 1960s brought racial strife, rise in crime, increased divorce rate, the counterculture and the drug scene. Tragedy of tragedies was the removal of prayer and Bible reading from our schools, which undermined the moral and biblical heritage of our country.

During this same time, Campus Crusade for Christ began interdenominational evangelism training in individual churches, citywide seminars and conferences at our headquarters at Arrowhead Springs, California. I gave two messages. One was called "Marriage: Moonlight or Mayhem" and the other was called "Women: Fearful or Forceful." The first message was about the Spirit-filled life in the husband-wife relationship. The second message encouraged women to be "salt and light" in their homes and community to make a difference where they live.

I became active in my own community through the women's club and the PTA and helped to initiate local programs that might have an opportunity to make a difference in people's lives where I lived.

Two news reports were an inspiration to me. The first was a group of Brazilian women who threatened to fill the airport runways should another international political entity try a takeover through influencing their national election process.

The other encouraging report came from Indianapolis, Indiana. Women had mobilized in their city to work with the police and city officials to encourage action that resulted in a reduced crime rate. As a result of these reports, I asked myself and others, "What effect could Christian women have on a community if *we* were mobilized?" Interestingly enough, in both of these reports, action had begun in the church.

In 1968, while speaking at a women's conference in London, Ontario, I was inspired early one morning with the idea of a movement called "Women Concerned" and felt this was something that maybe God would like me to initiate. When I returned home and shared this idea with my husband and children, our 14-year-old son said, "All this family needs is a 'crusading' mother." I knew this was not the time in my children's lives that I should begin such a movement, but I did often refer to the idea and found that when I shared it, women were very responsive.

In 1969, I was asked, along with Millie Dienert, to chair a women's luncheon at the American Congress on Evangelism held in Minneapolis, and sponsored by the Billy Graham Association. In preparation for that event, we put together a four-page action sheet to give the women, listing specific ways they could initiate involvement in their own communities.

After the meeting, I asked four women to join me to brainstorm the mobilization of Christian women to action in this country. Ruth Graham, Millie Dienert, Marian Lindsell, Alicia Davidson and I concluded that the answer was to mobilize them in prayer. How would we do it? That answer came several months later when Millie observed that one woman—Jean Reese, a pastor's wife—had marshaled 9,000 women to pray in preparation for the Billy Graham campaign in London. All this happened in three months' time and without the help of advertising or media.

On December 6, 1971, during my regular devotions, I was reading Acts 4 where Peter and John had just been released from prison. They sought the other disciples and joined them for a prayer meeting. Verse 24 describes how "the believers were united as they lifted their voices in prayer." They prayed for the leadership of the country and about the decadence of the day; they asked for boldness for themselves, and for God's mighty power to enable them to be adequate in proclaiming the gospel. At the end of that passage, in verse 32, it speaks of the believers being of one heart and mind. This passage spoke to my heart so specifically that I began to wonder what would happen if we would challenge Christian women to unite together in specific and strategic prayer in one heart and mind.

I called my four friends, the idea clicked and we formed "The Great Commission Prayer Crusade." The movement was launched when a local committee in my area requested that Ruth Graham speak for a women's prayer rally in the Los Angeles Sports Arena. Seven thousand came on February 24, 1972. Pastors and Christian leaders around the nation were very supportive and encouraging as I wrote to them about the idea. The Great Commission Prayer Crusade had become the prayer base for Explo '72, a national conference of students and adults held in the Cotton Bowl. It was the largest multiday conference of its kind ever held in the United States, where 80,000 attended nightly and 250,000 attended on the last day, a Saturday.

We followed the strategy of Jean Reese of London in recruiting zip code captains, church and neighborhood coordinators. We prepared two manuals. One was a city strategy and the other was a prayer-teaching guide. The result was prayer rallies and workshops in major cities around the country and a mobilization of a local prayer movement. Some are still in existence almost four decades later, perhaps under different names.

In an effort of communication and cooperation, I sought to bring together leaders of other movements. The first was Mr. Frank Insen of World Vision, and together we began to seek out others. In 1974, we held our first meeting at the newly purchased residence of the Christian Embassy in Washington, DC. Those attending were Mr. Insen, Dick Eastman, Millie Dienert, Evelyn Christenson and myself. A year later, we had discovered 70 prayer movements—much alike but also uniquely different. We called these prayer groups to come together in Washington, DC. As I remember, there were about 50 people present at that meeting. It was a wonderful time of sharing our desire for unity and support of each other. Prominent at that meeting was Dr. Harold Lindsell, then editor of *Christianity Today*.

In 1974, Billy Graham called world leaders together in Lausanne, Switzerland, for a conference on World Evangelization. I was invited to be one of three women with 50 male Christian leaders from around the world to form a continuation committee called "The Lausanne Committee for World Evangelization." This was a great thrill for me, and I was appointed to the Prayer Advisory Group. This provided the opportunity to implement ideas internationally that I had initiated in our country. From this, it was natural for me to call together the people with whom I had originally met in Washington to strategize on mobilizing prayer in the U.S.

Plans were being made for the 1976 Bicentennial, and we were very desirous to see a strong prayer emphasis take place in our country at that time. Representatives from Intercessors for America, founded by John Beckett; Heal Our Land musical by Jimmy and Carol Owens; and Wyatt Lipscomb, a lawyer active in prayer, from Garland, Texas, met with us. Norval Hadley replaced Mr. Insen with World Vision. Later, Joy and Jim Dawson from Youth With A Mission; Glenn Sheppard, representing the Southern Baptists; and Evelyn Christianson joined our committee. The commander of The Salvation Army became a member, as well as a representative from United Methodists.

We began to have prayer conferences in different cities, with encouraging results. Dr. Edwin Orr, an authority on spiritual awakenings, was a regular speaker. Dr. Stephen Olford and Dr. E. V. Hill joined our conference platform speakers, participating with committee members who also conducted workshops.

In 1981, the North American Lausanne Committee sponsored a Festival of Evangelism in Kansas City. The prayer committee met for months in prayer support and preparation for that event. We planned and taught a daily plenary session where prayer instruction and guidance were given for united, specific and strategic prayer. This was a significant contribution and gave a unique dimension to that conference.

The committee debated about what our next step would be and decided to meet in July to determine our future. David Bryant, who had recently sensed a call from God to prayer, was invited to join us. A few weeks before that meeting, businessman Joe Mays, who was very active with Religious Heritage of America, approached me. He shared that the National Day of Prayer needed some person or group to give it direction and suggested that I be the person to take that initiative. I shared this with the prayer committee, which had no specific name to this point. I had attended two National Day of Prayer events in Washington, DC, and a prayer rally held in Constitution Hall.

The history of the National Day of Prayer actually began on April 17, 1952, when a bill initiated by Mr. Conrad Hilton of Hilton Hotels and Senator Frank Carlson of Kansas was passed mandating that the president of the United States set aside an appropriate day each year, other than Sunday, as a National Day of Prayer.

It was inspired by a historically recorded statement of President Eisenhower's, saying that he doubted the day would be significantly observed until it was set as a definite date. It became my personal goal to see that happen.

As we prayed together as a committee, we felt God leading us to take on this project. We decided to call ourselves the National Prayer Committee. We contacted the White House to share our burden for the National Day of Prayer (NDP) and to make ourselves available to promote the event. The Public

Liaison office gave us their approval and encouraged us to become a task force. Our first event was held at Constitution Hall in Washington, DC, on the first Thursday of May 1983. The response was overwhelming. Vice President George Bush was our featured guest speaker, along with Dr. Lloyd Ogilvie, pastor of Hollywood Presbyterian Church and chaplain of the U.S. Senate.

Each year, President Reagan had taken significant steps to promote the National Day of Prayer. Before the end of his administration, it seemed appropriate that we, as a committee (after five years of leading a task force to promote the National Day of Prayer), take steps toward making the NDP a permanent date. As a result of the friends I had made who were in positions of influence in Washington, DC, and the experiences God had allowed me to have, I was encouraged to put a plan into action.

The first person I contacted was Senator Strom Thurmond (Republican), and I asked him what to do. He suggested I contact a Democrat and a Republican senator and a Democrat and a Republican congressman to be co-sponsors. Our son Brad, a political science major and former employee of Senator Bill Armstrong, mapped out a strategy for me, which I followed.

In July 1987, Senator Thurmond took the initiative to word the bill and then introduced it to the Senate Judicial Committee. It became bill S.1378, "which amended the current law establishing the National Day of Prayer, to set aside the first Thursday of May as the day on which the National Day of Prayer will be observed annually."

With his encouragement, we proceeded to contact the other men: Congressman Tony Hall (Democrat-Ohio) and Congressman Carlos Moorhead (Republican-California); Senator

Howard Heflin (Democrat-Alabama) joined Senator Thurmond (Republican-South Carolina). In turn, each man began to recruit his colleagues to join us as co-sponsors. Senator Bill Armstrong (Republican-Colorado) worked diligently, as did Congressman Frank Wolf (Republican-Virginia) and Congressman Bob Garcia (Democrat-New York). Many other senators (10) and congressmen (90) of both parties signed, giving their endorsements.

We began a race against time as the month of March approached. We knew it would be the last month for us to take action. Congressman Tony Hall put his aide Marty Rendon to work, almost exclusively, on this project.

Susan McDonald Sorensen, assisting in my office, was tenacious, tireless and very efficient in taking initiative and carrying out instructions. She and Marty Rendon worked closely together to accomplish much of the behind-the-scenes action—making phone calls, writing letters and following through on details.

We knew it would take nothing short of a miracle for this bill to get passed. It needed to go through the Congressional and Senate Committees, passed by Congress and then the Senate before it could be presented to the President.

We began to pray by name for the members of these committees. The Judiciary Committee in the Senate and the Committee on the Post Office and Civil Service in the House each had to release this bill for vote. After the Senate took action, we discovered on a Monday afternoon that the next meeting for the House Committee would be on Wednesday of that week. That was the last time the committee would meet before May 5, the National Day of Prayer in 1988. Marty was able to get word to the secretary of the committee on Tuesday morning, requesting that the National Day of Prayer bill be brought before the committee on Wednesday.

The secretary impatiently telephoned the NDP office, complaining that it was impossible to do what was requested. Susan was patient and gracious, explaining our goal. A few hours later the secretary of the committee called back with a very sweet attitude, saying that the bill would be presented the next day.

We encouraged coordinators in local and state areas to contact their congressman to support the passage of this bill. Rabbi Habermann and Rabbi Tannenbaum were a great help in contacting the Jewish members of Congress and the Senate. The bill passed unanimously in the Senate and, a few days later, in the House.

Now it needed the final recording and printing before it could be signed. It had to be followed daily because bills are not usually processed so quickly. It was not until 4:00 P.M. on Wednesday that we were given final confirmation that it would be signed in the Oval Office the next day. It was signed into law on May 8, 1988.

Anticipated to be present for the signing were: President Reagan (of course); me (chair); Pat Boone (co-chair); Susan Sorensen (National Coordinator); Congressman Tony Hall (D) (sponsor of the bill); Congressman Frank Wolf (R); Congressman Carlos Moorhead (R) (co-sponsor of the bill); Senate Chaplain Dr. Richard Halverson; House Chaplain William Ford; Senator Howard Heflin (D) (co-sponsor for the Senate); Rabbi Joshua Habermann; Father John O'Connor; Dr. Jerry C. Nims (National Advisor); Gladys Harrington, who presented President Reagan with a nine-volume, handwritten copy of the Bible written by citizens of Tulsa, Oklahoma, that was begun in 1983 as a part of the Year of the Bible. Because of short notice, only President Reagan, me, Pat Boone, Susan Sorensen, Congressman Carlos Moorhead, Rabbi Joshua Habermann, Father John O'Connor, Dr. Jerry C. Nims and Gladys Harrington were able to be present for the actual signing.

Praise God for the united hearts who prayed and worked so diligently to bring about such a significant day—a yearly celebration of our biblical heritage in this nation!

Now that you have read a little about my history and personal involvement in prayer ministry, I want to shift the focus to you.

Today, we are blessed with such sophisticated means of communication and can instantly get in touch with anyone, anywhere, anytime. When I was reviewing the material used for so many years in Campus Crusade, I realized that the principles have not changed. We, as God's people, have always had Instant Messaging with our heavenly Father and, fortunately, we are not dependent on natural power sources.

I want to focus the rest of this book on the practical aspects of prayer so that you can personally apply its power to your life. The material in this book has been tested in many diverse environments, and there are personal testimonies of prayer's life-changing impact around the world. But first, it is imperative that you understand how to allow God to work in you. What I've written would be of no value to you if you did not sense the reality of the Spirit of God moving in your life.

Chapter 2

Prayer Begins with a Relationship

Do you remember when you spoke your first word? Probably not. The development of speech is so amazing; and when you think about the vocabulary of a toddler, it is no less than miraculous. The capacity of the human brain to formulate speech, remember an ever-expanding vocabulary and communicate effectively is the essence of our humanity and the main quality that allows us to be civilized. Our precious heavenly Father created us to have the capacity to communicate with the spoken word.

Speech is the oldest academic discipline (tracing its roots to Aristotle). It is our speech that allows us to develop relationships with others. I believe that one of the greatest deterrents to effective prayer is that we have difficulty understanding the communication of the Spirit. I know that God is not cold or indifferent, and He desires to have an intimate relationship with me. As I reflect on the years of my life and how my communication with God has deepened, I can testify to you that if you will pursue God wholeheartedly, your communication with Him will become as necessary as the air you breathe.

The Bible tells us that He is love and that He never stops desiring an ever-closer relationship with each one of His children. God has a wonderful plan for every single one of us, no matter what our circumstances may be. The most beautiful part of the wonderful plan is to know Him intimately—to enjoy a deep and fulfilling relationship unlike any human relationship we will ever have. God demonstrated the depth of His love by sacrifice. He put aside His power, rights and splendor as Creator of the universe to rescue us from the consequences of our own sin. He left the majesty of heaven to become incarnated as a tiny, helpless baby—He came to the world He had created, to a universe He ruled, and made Himself known to us as Jesus of Nazareth.

Jesus, fully God and fully human, lived among us and demonstrated through His life and teachings just how we are supposed to live. He was the Word of God made flesh. Then, on the cross where men crucified Him, He paid the death penalty for our sins. He took on our punishment so that we might be spared to enjoy eternal life and an intimate relationship with Him now and forever. This was made possible when He rose from the dead as the "first fruit" of this new order, just as we, too, will rise again.

Then something incredible and marvelous happened. When Jesus returned to heaven to sit at the right hand of the Father, He made a way to remain among us as long as we live on this earth. He released His Holy Spirit to come and live inside each one of His followers. In that way, we have the mind and the Spirit of Jesus living within us.

That is why He told His disciples that it was better for them that He leave this world (see John 16:7). They had enjoyed only the physical presence of Jesus among them. Now, and for all time, He is among us in the deepest and most powerful way, living within our hearts. We have Jesus' counsel, comfort, strength and friendship with us wherever we go, and nothing we, or anyone, can do will ever take it away. The Bible tells us this presence of His Holy Spirit is a preview, a foretaste, of the wonderful fellowship that lies ahead of us when we join Him in eternity.

The Key to Daily Fellowship with God

Why is it that God is with us and within us, yet so many of us live with little awareness of His presence? We face life's problems without taking advantage of His wisdom. We cope with crises without calling upon the limitless strength that He has to offer us. Have you made that mistake in your own life? Why do you think this happens?

It certainly is not because God wants it to be so. Psalm 145:18 tells us, "The LORD is close to all who call on him, yes, to all who call on him sincerely." That means that the Lord longs to maintain an intimate relationship with us. I believe the key word in that verse is "sincerely." How sincere are you in calling upon the Lord? Do you really want to have a daily dependence upon Him? Or are you simply looking for instant help from the immediate problem of the day? Do you wish to partake in a rich and full relationship with the King of all kings? Or are you concerned that He might interfere with the way you want to run your life?

Those impure motives will never cause God to stop reaching out to you, but they will make it much more difficult for you to know the fullness of His love and power. Only when you finally come to a sincere desire for Him, as the psalm indicates, will you discover what He has wanted you to have all along.

The Lord desires daily fellowship with you through the Holy Spirit, whom He sent to indwell each of us. The moment you accept God's gift of salvation and receive Christ into your life, He enters your heart in the person of the Holy Spirit. Though you may not always be aware of Him, He takes permanent residence inside you. If you are a Christian, the Spirit of Christ remains within you every moment of every day.

When Christ walked on planet Earth physically, His time was limited. He could only be in one place at one time, and spend that time with only a few people. Living as a man limited His physical reach. But now, as He lives within each of us in the person of the Holy Spirit, there are no limits on our access to Him. Any time, any place, every believer can live in the wonderful presence of God. And we have the same Friend and Comforter the first Christians had some 2,000-plus years ago.

Maybe you have never heard about what is available to you through the Holy Spirit; or maybe you have simply forgotten. But if you have ever thought, *If only I could talk to Jesus as the disciples were able to do! If only I could sit at His feet, hear His teachings and see His miracles. Life would be so much simpler and so much less frightening if I had God in the flesh right here beside me,* then you need to understand that what you have now is so much better and is ever present. Yes, it would be wonderful to look into the eyes of Jesus and ask Him the deepest questions of your life. But you can, through faith, look into His face and have an intimate relationship with Him right now. As your passion to communicate with Him intensifies, your spiritual maturity will grow. And the opposite is true. That is why some young believers are so spiritually mature and yet some who have walked with Christ for many years may remain spiritually immature.

"Lord, Help Us to Pray!"

Visualize the scene that opens Luke 11: Jesus is caught up in deep prayer, barely conscious of the disciples who have gathered to watch Him with fascination. Imagine what those disciples saw, heard and felt. Here was a man praying as no one had ever been seen or heard to pray. In those days, the Pharisees offered prayers that were public, pompous and predictable. They mouthed a long stream of "vain repetitions," as Jesus called them. Prayer was a "town square" demonstration of one's religiosity. It was also one-way communication, for God remained silent during this period; He had not powerfully spoken or dealt with His people since the time of the prophets. Prayer had become an empty, meaningless exercise.

But here was Jesus, who prayed at all times—who slipped away each morning for prayer, sought God in the midst of each important development and seemed to have an incredible intimacy with His Father. This kind of prayer resembled a meeting with a beloved friend. So the disciples watched with fascination as He prayed in Luke 11:1. One of them could no longer contain his desire to experience something so wonderful. As Jesus finished praying, the disciple cried out, "Lord, teach us to pray!"

Have you ever felt like that? Have you ever commiserated with the feeling that Ziggy, the cartoon character, portrayed when he stood on the mountain peak and called out to heaven, "Am I to be put on hold for the rest of my life?" All of us feel a deep craving not simply to talk to God, but also to talk *with* God. We have no desire for the mere trappings of prayer; we want the real thing. And each of us has felt the disappointment of dry, dead prayer when our words seem to bounce off the ceiling and return to us unheard.

We read books on prayer. We try new methods. We wonder if there is some hidden formula or secret that will provide the key to powerful prayer. But in reality there is only one secret, and His name is the Holy Spirit. He carries us beyond our weaknesses and limitations. He carries us directly into the incredible, loving presence of God Himself.

Our Helper in Prayer

Prayer is the most intimate communication ever devised. It is heart-to-heart, spirit-to-Spirit communication between us—the created—and our Creator. Prayer is conversation with God—asking Him for guidance, praising Him for His goodness, sharing with Him our needs and the needs of others and knowing by faith that He hears and will grant our requests.

God longs to meet with us in prayer, because it represents the difference between our truly *knowing* Him versus merely knowing *about* Him. You could spend your life studying the works of all the great theologians, and read every worthy Christian book ever written about God. You could become an expert on all the facts that have been revealed about Him. But still you would not *know* God, not even remotely, unless you communed with Him in prayer. A six-year-old girl who, with childlike faith, kneels at bedtime could know the Lord more intimately than you, for even her childish prayer is more intimate and personal than mere theological facts and doctrine. Real, living prayer is only possible through praying in the Spirit.

As you live in the Spirit, prayer is the foundation of your days and your way of life. As you awaken each morning, you invite the Lord to work in and through you. You pray that everything that comes to your mind will be filtered through the blood of Christ and the Word of God. You turn your thoughts to praise, prayer and thanksgiving. What an honor to be able to bring your concerns to the One who made you and holds the universe together!

As long as we can pray, there is hope in all things. If a family member is spiritually lost without Christ, prayer can make the difference. If a boss overwhelms us with work, we have a place to take our concerns. If we are disappointed and heartbroken over a struggling marriage, we need never give up. We know there is always prayer.

Here is a verse to cherish in your heart: "The effective prayer of a righteous man can accomplish much" (Jas. 5:16, *NASB*). Intercessory prayer (praying for the needs of others) offered in a righteous spirit can actually influence the course of history. It has happened many times in the past; in fact, I believe it happens every day.

In 1934, just to name one example, a farmer asked a group of his friends to come to his farm and spend the day in prayer. He was just an ordinary farmer. As the men prayed together, they felt compelled to ask God to raise up a man from their city to carry the gospel to the ends of the earth. There was no immediate answer, but the farmer's teenage son became a believer during the crusade that year. Although you would not recognize the farmer's name, you most likely have heard of his son, Billy Graham.

That farmer was a world-shaker, because God answered his simple prayer. Never forget that you have every opportunity that farmer had.

The Spirit's Role in Prayer

In the days when the Temple was still in use in Jerusalem, only the high priest was allowed to enter the holy of holies to atone for the sins of the people—and this only once a year. When he entered that sacred place, he came into the very presence of God. In that day, an individual's closest encounter with God would be to interact with the priest . . . on the public side of the curtain.

Yet, as believers, now we can go past the curtain. We can approach the eternal, infinite Creator God of the universe any time of the day, any day of the year. Why? Because of the self-less sacrifice of our Savior, Jesus, when He died on the cross for our sins. Now, we can "boldly enter heaven's Most Holy Place" (Heb. 10:19).

The Holy Spirit is the one who eagerly clasps your hand and walks you into God's throne room. "Now all of us, both Jews and Gentiles, may come to the Father through the same Holy Spirit because of what Christ has done for us" (Eph. 2:18).

Doesn't that fact change the way you look at prayer? It is the most precious, valuable privilege we could ever receive. We should take advantage of it at every available instant, and with unparalleled eagerness: "So let us come boldly to the throne of our gracious God. There we will receive his mercy, and we will find grace to help us when we need it" (Heb. 4:16).

The Holy Spirit does a number of wonderful things to help us with prayer.

The Holy Spirit Prompts Us to Pray

Have you ever felt that little nudge? You may be going about your business, your mind on many earthly matters, when you sense a little mental tug. You feel the urge to pray about a particular matter or person. This impression could even wake you in the middle of the night. There have been many Christians who, in various situations, were led to pray for a loved one or friend, only to find that this person was in a dangerous situation at that very moment.

The Holy Spirit Guides Our Prayers

The Holy Spirit also molds and shapes our prayers, helping them to be effective and consistent with the will of God. He guides us through the needs of the day, through the emotions of the hour and through recollections of people we care about. He helps us pray for all the many things we need to bring before the Father.

As He does this, something wonderful happens. The Spirit brings our desires into conformity with God's will. It may be that you have encountered a very difficult situation in your life. You feel a great deal of anxiety, and naturally you ask God for a change in the circumstances. But as the days and prayers move by, you find that the circumstances remain the same while your attitude has utterly changed: You suddenly comprehend how God could use someone like you in just such a setting. You realize that He didn't want to help you *out* of this mess, but to help you *through* it. More miracles happen in the midst of a crisis than when we are fleeing from it.

God's Spirit guides your prayer over time until you are asking for Him to lead you rather than remove you from the situation. The Bible assures us, "God is working in you, giving you the desire to obey him and the power to do what pleases him" (Phil. 2:13).

You pray for God to change things, but in the process, you are the one changed! It works much like the anchor on a ship. When men take hold of the chain to the anchor, their efforts pull the boat toward the anchor, rather than the anchor up to the boat. In the same way, when we pray, tugging at the "chain" of prayer pulls us toward God. We are moved gradually into His awesome presence where our hearts are transformed by the power of His love.

Prayer keeps you anchored, in every sense of the word. When you feel the pull of the Spirit to turn your heart toward prayer, you can be joyful in realizing that you will be even closer to the wonderful purposes of God by the time you have finished.

The Spirit guides our prayers; and best of all, He guides our spirits toward God.

The Holy Spirit Intercedes for Us in Prayer

Here is one of the most remarkable promises and supernatural ministries of the Spirit when we pray: "In the same way, the Spirit helps us in our weakness. We do not know what we ought to pray for, but the Spirit himself intercedes for us with groans that words cannot express" (Rom. 8:26, *NIV*). I have always found this to be a tremendously encouraging truth.

You may say, "But I lack the knowledge of how to pray!" Every believer should learn to pray biblically, for praying in agreement with God's Word is vital. God's character is unchanging, and He acts on our behalf in accordance with His Word. If you understand the promises of God, you can claim those promises when you pray. If you feel uncertain what to say to God in prayer, read a passage of Scripture as your prayer.

However, that is not the major issue, because the Spirit prays for those things we lack the understanding to pray for. He also expresses the depth of emotion that we might feel if we could see with complete spiritual clarity. He helps us pray beyond our many limitations. Knowing this makes me all the more eager to pray, as I am sure it does you.

The Holy Spirit knows us better than we know ourselves. He understands our desires, our fears, our strengths and weaknesses. He knows what we need before we even know to ask for it. The Holy Spirit, the third person of the Trinity, knows the mind of God. "He who searches our hearts knows the mind of the Spirit, because the Spirit intercedes for the saints in accordance with God's will" (Rom. 8:27, *NIV*). Who better to speak to our heavenly Father for us than the Holy Spirit?

We have so many limitations, so many failings. But we can be joyful in the realization that the Spirit of God stands in the gap, interceding for us. Your prayers are more powerful than you can possibly realize, because He enhances and enlarges them.

The Holy Spirit Leads Us in Prayerful Worship

Prayer, of course, is more than a flood of requests. The Spirit helps us to praise and exalt God when we pray. He gives us the realization of the awesomeness of God. He leads us to comprehend just how infinite, how majestic and how sovereign He truly is, and then, as a result, we can do nothing other than worship in spirit and in truth.

The Spirit frees us from the monotony and dryness of dead prayer by filling our hearts with the wonderful music of true worship. Music begins where words leave off, and sometimes the only way to express our feelings about God's greatness is through the transcendence of melody and verse. Paul urges us, "Let the Holy Spirit fill and control you. Then you will sing psalms and hymns and spiritual songs among yourselves, making music to the Lord in your hearts" (Eph. 5:18-19). The Spirit makes worship a natural and joyful thing, not merely at church, but wherever we may be.

You will find that prayer is the spark that sets worship aflame. You may begin a devotional time with a mood nowhere close to that of worship. But then, as you praise your Lord for His many benefits, as you thank Him for all He has done in your life, as you realize all the many requests you are allowed to bring before Him—what can you do but exalt and magnify His name? You will break out in song within your heart, for words will not be enough. Then you will feel mentally, emotionally and spiritually refreshed for having worshiped.

The Spirit, in His wisdom, knew you needed that. So He became your worship leader.

In each of these ways—guidance, intercession and worship—the Spirit makes the difference in our prayers. Now let us look at some guidelines for praying in the Spirit.

How to Pray in the Spirit

You have just read about some of the many ministries of the Holy Spirit in prayer. But what kind of prayer allows you to sense the transforming presence of God? There are a number of considerations to remember that do away with common misunderstandings about prayer.

Too often, we feel that God is most impressed by eloquent words or the length of a prayer. Yet, He has no particular regard for either of these. A prayer from the heart, whatever the wording or the brevity, is what He looks for. He wants us to pray in the very midst of our life's circumstances and emotions. These are the times when we are likely to lift up the most heartfelt prayers.

Paul wrote, "Pray in the Spirit on all occasions with all kinds of prayers and requests" (Eph. 6:18, *NIV*). Your most effective prayers may come in the most unlikely places—but don't become so "informal" that you lose sight of the greatness and awesomeness of the One to whom you are praying. This brings us to the first suggestion for praying in the spirit.

Address God Respectfully

To pray in the Spirit is to pray with a reverent heart. We should never come before God without reverence and awe for who He is: "Since we are receiving a Kingdom that cannot be destroyed, let us be thankful and please God by worshiping him with holy fear and awe" (Heb. 12:28). "Fear" is a word that is often missing today from our understanding of a relationship with God, but I believe it refers to a surpassing sense of how awesome and holy God is. When we come to grips with these realities, we are humbled, and God rewards the humble. The prophet Isaiah proclaimed, "The high and lofty one who inhabits eternity, the Holy One, says this: 'I live in that high and holy place with those whose spirits are contrite and humble. I refresh the humble and give new courage to those with repentant hearts' " (Isa. 57:15).

We also feel joyfully thankful when we pray as the Holy Spirit leads. Do you spend as much time expressing gratitude as you do asking for more blessings? If not, this is a sign that you are not truly praying in the Spirit, who will usher you into God's presence and fill your heart with thankfulness. You should have times of prayer that are completely given to thanking Him. The next time you cannot feel the presence of God, and you struggle to find an attitude of worship, spend some time expressing your gratitude. You will be amazed at how quickly your mood will change.

Initiate Transparent Conversation with God

Praying as the Spirit leads gives you the freedom to be yourself. As you have already read on a previous page, James 5:16 tells us, "the effective prayer of a *righteous* man can accomplish much" (*NASB*, emphasis added). If you have confessed your sin, there is no obstacle between you and God. You can be completely open and honest, telling Him exactly what is on your heart. "If our conscience is clear, we can come to God with bold confidence. And we will receive whatever we request because we obey him and do the things that please him" (1 John 3:21-22). The key to answered prayer, then, is being in harmony with God. As you come into His presence and know Him more fully, you will experience that harmony.

No relationship can be deep and strong without honest communication, and your relationship with God is no different. You will experience wonderful liberation when you learn what it is like to be completely honest with God, with no shame or striving to be something you are not. You can worship Him "in spirit and in truth" (John 4:23), as Jesus told the woman at the well. When you pray in the Spirit, you will be transparent with God. He knows all that is inside you anyway.

Speak to God as your Father, your dearest Friend. Speak simply and honestly with Him, telling Him your deepest concerns and emotions. Open up to Him with full transparency.

Declare Your Confidence in God

There is no need to come before God with hesitation and timidity, as if you lack trust in His power. You are praying to the Creator and Sustainer of the universe. If you are praying as the Spirit directs, you can confidently come before Him with your requests.

This means fully realizing your dependence upon Him. One of the most essential effects of prayer is the way it reminds each of us how helpless we are apart from Him. We must submit ourselves to His lordship every day, because our spirits are rebellious and stubborn. As we come before God, we acknowledge our limitations. We cast ourselves upon His mercy and His power, affirming that we can do no good thing on our own.

Then, having felt our own helplessness, we express faith in His worthiness. Praying as the Spirit directs you strengthens your faith that though you are weak, He is strong. As you pray, you *believe* that He will act as He desires. You believe that He will work through you. You believe that He is totally sovereign. Your faith is strengthened when you pray in the Spirit and you begin to live in the confident assurance that He is Lord, and that He is working in your world and working through you. Praying in the power of the Holy Spirit always leads to greater confidence and hope in God.

Perseverance matters in prayer. Faith that God will act is not the same as faith that God will act today, tomorrow or whenever your schedule dictates. He wants us to pray without ceasing, to keep praying with persistence. He knows that the discipline of sustained prayer is good for us. God gave my husband, Bill Bright, a vision in 1945 to produce a film on the life of Jesus. That vision became a reality 33 years later. God gave him a vision to train world leaders. That vision became a reality 25 years later.

We do not serve a God of convenience, but a God of perfect timing—a timing we usually will not know in advance. So keep on keeping on as you pray in the Spirit with faith and endurance. Never give up!

Prayer Reveals His Power

I believe that the greatest revelation of God's power in the world comes through the vehicle of prayer guided by the Holy Spirit. Prayer, often with fasting, accomplishes what nothing else will. It softens hearts. It calls friends and enemies to repentance. It reaches far beyond the borders of our mundane life to the other side of the globe and to generations yet unborn. It demolishes the devil's strongholds. Most important of all, it draws us into intimate communion with our awesome God, who is manifest in His magnificent glory through the prayer of His children.

There are so many true stories that illustrate the glorification of God and His power through the prayers of faithful believers that an entire library would be needed to contain them. Let me share one story.

In the mid 1800s, the great Scottish medical missionary David Livingstone feared for his life. As the sun set on his small camp in the interior of Africa, he knew the local tribe planned to attack that night and kill him and all of those by his side. Even in the midst of these warnings, Livingstone was strangely filled with peace. God was with him, and God could always be trusted. That night, Livingstone slept without anxiety—and his camp was unthreatened.

Two years later, a miracle happened: the chief of that hostile tribe became a Christian. Livingstone was eager to learn the story of why the tribe had never attacked on that memorable evening. The chief confirmed to him that an uprising had indeed been planned. They had left their settlement with weapons, anger and the intent to kill. But as the tribe approached Livingstone's camp, they had been surprised by what they saw: 47 mighty warriors guarding the place where the famous explorer slept.

Livingstone was shocked to hear this story two years later, because he knew there had been no guards. What was the truth?

On a visit home to England, he found out. Livingstone was informed that on that night of crisis two years earlier, across the ocean in Scotland, 47 church members had gathered, drawn by the Spirit, to pray fervently for Livingstone. Those prayer warriors stood watch over Livingstone before almighty God, and his life was spared.

When we are caught up in the Spirit to pray before God, incredible things happen all around us. We release His miraculous power to a world that has forgotten how powerful God is. Forty-seven believers, deep in prayer, were enough to turn back a murderous attack on another continent. What would happen in this world if all of God's children became prayer warriors, available to the call of the Spirit to lift up His name and His purposes? How would your life change if you began to pray in the manner described in this chapter?

Prayer begins and ends my day, filling it with faith and joy. I have seen the amazing power of God time and again because I prayed as the Spirit directed, and I know you can do the same. Can there be any better time than the present to begin to pray this way? What about this very moment?

It is time for all Christians to mobilize in prayer and put an end to a dead, dry prayer life. Communing with God is the ultimate adventure, and it is available today, tomorrow and every moment we draw breath.

Chapter 3

Praying in Accordance with Scriptural Principles

In the pages that follow, I offer practical principles that have worked for me for many years. There is nothing original or exclusive about this information. Many others have used these principles too, and we have recorded testimonies over the years of the amazing power of the effectual fervent prayer of believers. If you will accept prayer as a basic spiritual discipline and commit to create some structure for your prayer life, I can state with complete confidence that you will experience the presence of the almighty God and experience Him actively involved in your life. Let me give you one example of how God's presence and mighty power accomplished the unimaginable because of the increased and persistent prayers of people across our nation and the world.

In 1971, God gave us the strategy for a movement to inform, unite and accelerate prayer resources in the church, in Christian organizations, in Bible classes and other established prayer groups, and to develop new prayer resources, especially in neighborhoods, businesses and on campuses. This movement came to be known as "The Great Commission Prayer Crusade," a ministry of Campus Crusade for Christ.

People who were deeply concerned about the moral and spiritual values of society and were eager to know God's direction so that they could take action responded in large numbers across the United States and in other countries. We recorded many dramatic answers to prayer in the lives of individuals, families, neighborhoods, cities and, we believe, in our nation, as a result of united, specific prayer.

Although my husband, Bill, and I began to pray for the Soviet Union in 1946, it wasn't until 1978, at the height of the Cold War, that Bill was invited by the Soviet government, at the request of the church, to tour 8 cities, and he spoke 18 times. Many Russian people indicated a response to the gospel.

Years later, we were able to arrange a premiere showing of the *Jesus* film in Moscow. Nine of the 11 government ministers and other top leaders came to the event. Following the showing, the Minister of Education asked if we would give videotapes to 135,000 Soviet schools. Of course we agreed. Consequently, God opened the doors to train thousands of teachers in the truths of God's Word who then trained thousands more to reach millions of students with the gospel—all at the government's expense.

There is nothing too big for us to attempt for the glory of God! If our hearts and motives are pure, and what we do is faithful to the Word of God, He hears and will do more than we ask or even dare to hope to accomplish.

Properly Exercising the Power of Prayer

Prayer is the Christian's most powerful weapon against wickedness and the powers of darkness, yet it is perhaps the most neglected facet of Christian worship—probably because people do not know how to pray according to the Scripture's teaching.

In an effort to unite individuals and groups to pray, we discovered that people are relatively easy to motivate for an urgent crisis or emergency issue. But after a few meetings, interest wanes for many because persistent prayers seem mechanical, repetitious and unscriptural. When we analyzed the problems in personal and group prayer, we concluded that one of the greatest needs of our day is to teach people how to pray.

For prayer to be relevant, there are certain qualifications on the part of the believer, and a creative application of scriptural methods and ideas. I want to pass on to you some of the principles I have learned for personal and group prayer, as well as for the acceleration of prayer in the local church. This very practical information is for every person who wishes to enhance his or her personal prayer life, teach others to pray or accelerate prayer in the local church.

Examine Your Motivation

Most people would agree that we live in a time when there is more information regarding the power of prayer and the need for prayer than ever before in our history. Yet, with all the information available, we do not see many examples of personal holiness; and within the church, moral failure has become all too common. That's because prayerlessness results in the lack of a powerful spiritual life; but prayer based upon the Word of God is our greatest means of achieving personal holiness and moral strength.

When you pray for personal holiness, be prepared for God to refine you. As you honestly examine your motives for prayer, you will be cleansed in spirit and prepared for communion with your heavenly Father.

Then, when you learn to deal honestly with your motivation, you will learn how to worship and express adoration for God as the psalmists did. Your prayers will be more effective when you pray in accordance with Scripture. Your agreement with Scripture will make God very real to you as you experience answered prayer.

Scripture gives us a basis to pray with greater faith and confidence in God's promise to hear and answer our prayers as we apply the scriptural principles, and we definitely become more fruitful in our witness for Christ.

Guidelines for Praying Scripturally

To effectively communicate with God, you must begin by evaluating your relationship with Him. God listens when His children pray: "The Lord is watching His children, listening to their prayers" (1 Pet. 3:12, *TLB*).

We know that God is ready to hear those who worship Him and do His will: We know that "God doesn't listen to sinners, but he is ready to hear those who worship him and do his will" (John 9:31).

If you are not sure of your relationship with God, make sure. The only way that you become a child of God is by receiving His Son, Jesus Christ.

> But to all who believed him and accepted him, he gave the right to become children of God. They are reborn! This is not a physical birth resulting from human passion or plan, this rebirth comes from God (John 1:12-13).

> You are all children of God through faith in Christ Jesus (Gal. 3:26).

From this point on, I will refer you to many biblical passages. I encourage you to look up the passages and write out the ones that have special meaning to your circumstances.

God requires that we come to Him with a clean heart. So ask God to reveal any unconfessed sin in your life. Sin short-circuits your relationship with God.

Here is a list of some hindrances to prayer for you to personally consider.

- Selfishness and wrong motives (see Jas. 4:2-3)
- Lack of compassion (see Prov. 21:13)
- Lack of domestic harmony or peace with mate, children, relatives (see 1 Pet. 3:7)
- Pride (see Job 35:12-13)
- Disobedience (see 1 John 3:22)
- Lack of faith (see Jas. 5:15)
- Unforgiving spirit (see Matt. 5:23-25)
- Failure to ask according to God's will (see 1 John 5:14)
- Failure to know God's Word and to abide in Christ (see John 15:7)
- Hypocrisy (see Matt. 6:5)
- Wrong attitudes, impure thoughts, jealousy, guilt, worry, discouragement, frustration, aimlessness (see Gal. 5:19-21)
- Loss of first love (see Rev. 2:4)
- Lukewarmness (see Rev. 3:16)
- Critical attitude (see Matt. 7:1-5)

Confess all sin that God brings to your mind. He promises to cleanse and forgive you.

But if we confess our sins to him, he is faithful and just to forgive us and to cleanse us from every wrong (1 John 1:9).

Thank Him that He has forgiven all of your sins as He said He would. The very act of saying "thank You" demonstrates faith that pleases God. Don't let the memory of confessed sin trouble you again. You are clean in the sight of God.

Appropriate the filling of the Holy Spirit by faith and claim the promises of God. The Holy Spirit enables you to pray effectively.

The word "prayer" in Hebrew means two-way communication. Prayer is simply talking to God. Prayer involves a personal relationship, not a ritual. It is the greatest privilege of the believer. It is communion and fellowship with God that makes your relationship with Him more meaningful.

Please, dear ones, don't make prayer a difficult task. It is merely asking, seeking and knocking. God knew that blind Bartimaeus needed sight, but He waited for Bartimaeus to ask (see Mark 10:51). He knew that Hannah wanted a son (see 1 Sam. 1), and that Hezekiah needed deliverance from Sennacherib's armed might (see 2 Kings 19); yet, He waited for them to ask for their needs before He provided them.

Jesus enunciated this principle in Matthew 7:7-8:

> Keep on asking, and you will be given what you ask for. Keep on looking, and you will find. Keep on knocking, and the door will be opened. For everyone who asks, receives. Everyone who seeks, finds. And the door is opened to everyone who knocks.

Prayer is simply bringing your needs, and the needs of others, to your heavenly Father, who cares, knows, understands, listens and answers. As I write this sentence I realize there are people who will read it and not understand what I mean by *simply* bringing your needs to your heavenly Father. The need may be very grave, but the plea for God's help can be brief and simple. God honors our humble admissions of need and expressions of dependence upon Him.

> Trust in the LORD with all your heart; do not depend on your own understanding. Seek his will in all you do, and he will direct your paths (Prov. 3:5-6).

For the believer, prayer is not an option. God's Word instructs us to pray and to never stop praying (see 1 Thess. 5:17-18). In Luke 18:1-8, you can read the story that Jesus used as an example of God's response to persistent prayer.

Scripture tells us that our prayers glorify God: "You can ask for anything in my name, and I will do it, because the work of the Son brings glory to the Father. Yes, ask anything in my name, and I will do it!" (John 14:13-14). And God delights in our prayers: "The Lord hates the sacrifice of the wicked, but he delights in the prayers of the upright" (Prov. 15:8).

Our Lord Jesus Christ set a perfect example of prayer for us (see Matt. 6:9-14). Great religious leaders of the centuries have also set an example, and we have records of the results—leaders such as George Washington, the "Father of our Country" and first President of the United States, who once wrote, "Bless O Lord the whole race of mankind, and let the world be filled with the knowledge of Thee and Thy Son, Jesus Christ."[1]

Prayer is the Christian's secret weapon and the most powerful resource for change that God has given us (see John 14:12). You can help combat the spiritual warfare going on in the world through the power of prayer (see Eph. 6:10-20).

When we are aware of the need for personal change, and change within our families, our communities, our nation and our world, many times we try to take action, but with meager results, or we give up, thinking there is nothing we can do. But prayer calls forth God's power and might, enabling the believer to move the hand of God.

It is the same with my word. I send it out, and it always produces fruit. It will accomplish all I want it to, and it will prosper everywhere I send it (Isa. 55:11).

And we can be confident that he will listen to us whenever we ask him for anything in line with his will. And if we know he is listening when we make our requests, we can be sure that he will give us what we ask for (1 John 5:14-15).

The Christian who fails to pray for spiritual regeneration and moral reform is aiding the cause of the enemy. Your prayers cause God to influence a world that otherwise shuts Him out. So recognize with whom you are fighting and take out your most effective weapon—prayer:

For we are not fighting against people made of flesh and blood, but against the evil rulers and authorities of the unseen world, against those mighty powers of darkness who rule this world, and against wicked spirits in the heavenly realms (Eph. 6:12).

John Wesley said, "God does nothing but in answer to prayer." That means you must pray about everything! Pray for your physical needs. Pray for your spiritual growth, for wisdom, for more faith. Pray about anything that excites you, troubles you, frightens you, gladdens you, saddens you. Acknowledge your personal needs and tell them to God. Perhaps you need help with a particular attitude, with your reactions to life and people, with your lack of forbearance with others, for a lack of love, for your need to be encouraged. If you have a problem or are carrying burdens too intimate to share, tell your heavenly Father about it.

> Don't worry about anything; instead, pray about everything. Tell God what you need, and thank him for all he has done (Phil. 4:6-7).

The psalmist wrote, "I love the Lord because he hears me and answers my prayers. Because he bends down and listens, I will pray as long as I have breath!" (Ps. 116:1-2, *TLB*).

Pray for your personal relationships with family, friends, neighbors, business associates. Pray for your community, nation and world. Start recording your prayers so that you can see when He answers. The Prayer Journal in the back of this book will help you keep a record that you can go back to over and over again when you need encouragement or just a fresh perspective on how God is working in your life.

Pray Reverently

It is imperative to approach God with a correct attitude—with awe, reverence and thanksgiving. Reverence will come when you realize that you are praying to almighty God—to the creator of heaven and earth, your King and merciful Father. An audience with the King is always a privilege. So approach Him with awe and respect. When you reverence Him, it is easy to pray thankfully.

Scripture commands you to always give thanks for all things. You can do that when you remember that He loves you, He saved you and He has your best interests at heart.

Give thanks for everything to God the Father in the name of our Lord Jesus Christ (Eph. 5:20).

Pray Boldly and with Vision

Our God is a great God and what we pray for is limited only by the depth of our faith. Scripture instructs us to approach the throne of God boldly (see Heb. 4:16). He can do the impossible in response to prayer if you pray for the miraculous and the supernatural. You can claim victory in Jesus Christ's name.

Pray Expectantly

When we pray, our heart is filled with an intense desire for that prayer's fulfillment. James 5:16 says that the effectual fervent prayer of a righteous man availeth much. Pray in faith, believing that God answers prayer. But recognize that God answers prayer in three ways: yes, no and wait. Any time a prayer is not answered as requested, God has a better plan. Praise and thank Him in advance for His answer.

Your Prayers Reflect What You Truly Believe

Belief is vital to faith—it counts the answer as though it has already arrived. Appropriating the answer connotes an attitude of expectancy in which the person who prays waits with a heart of confidence, accepting the gift as though it were already his possession. "Listen to me! You can pray for anything, and if you believe, you will have it" (Mark 11:24).

Consider the apostles and disciples who waited with great expectancy, for they had been told to tarry until endowed with power from on high (see Acts 1:8; 2).

In my book *In His Hands,* I define faith as "believing in that which is humanly impossible apart from a supernatural work of God." What we believe defines our faith.

When you pray, claim the authority you have in the name of the Lord Jesus Christ and in the power of His shed blood. With Him, you are co-crucified, co-buried, co-resurrected, co-ascended and co-seated at the right hand of the Father. So pray with authority.

Scriptural Admonitions Concerning Prayer

All prayer, as well as all acts and thoughts in life, should glorify God. The truly genuine, effective prayer life must be firmly rooted in a desire to glorify God; the prayer that does not will fail. God receives the glory when we pray for individuals to receive Christ, and when we make other requests that demonstrate His faithfulness.

Pray in the Name of the Lord Jesus Christ

Prayer exists for the benefit of those who have received Christ. To be on praying ground you must be able to come to God in Jesus' name because you acknowledge Him as Lord and Savior. John 16:23-24 makes this quite clear:

> At that time you won't need to ask me for anything. The truth is, you can go directly to the Father and ask him, and he will grant your request because you use my name. You haven't done this before. Ask, using my name, and you will receive, and you will have abundant joy.

God both hears and answers prayer offered according to His will. When your prayer is subordinated to the will of God, then all circumstances of life conform to the promise of Scripture: "And we know that God causes everything to work together for the good of those who love God and are called according to his purpose for them" (Rom. 8:28).

Pray in faith, believing that you have the answer. We must believe that God is able and willing to do what we ask (see Matt. 21:22). To be effectual, all prayer must be asked in faith:

It is impossible to please God without faith. Anyone who wants to come to him must believe that there is a God and that he rewards those who sincerely seek him (Heb. 11:6).

Become an Intercessor

To intercede is to pray with a "heart concern for others in which one stands between them and God, making request on their behalf."[2]

Identify those for whom you pray and seek God's sovereign perspective as you intercede. The enemy of our souls is powerless against intercessory prayer. "The greatest thing anyone can do for God and for man is to pray. It is not the only thing, but it is the chief thing."[3]

Pray for events and circumstances as well as for individuals.

Pray Persistently

God answers persistent prayer. If you want to be greatly encouraged about the power of faith in persistent prayer, get hold of a biography of missionary and orphanage founder George Müller. At the beginning of his ministry, Müller began persistently praying for the salvation of five friends. The first one accepted Christ after 5 years, the second and third after 10 years, the fourth man after 25 years, and the fifth man came to know Christ two years after Müller's death. Müller had prayed for 52 years for this man. God is faithful to His promises (see 2 Pet. 3:9).

Pray Specifically

Pray specifically in order to see specific answers. God becomes a greater reality to us when we receive answers to specific prayers; and answers to our specific prayers give us great opportunity to witness of God's grace.

Pray Creatively

Use various reminders to help you pray, such as the acronym ACTS, which stands for adoration, confession, thanksgiving and supplication (see a more in-depth explanation in this chapter under the subhead "Assignments for Creative Prayer"). Pray creatively to overcome dryness, weariness, distraction, mind-wandering and mechanical ritual. It is normal to pray for urgent needs; however, our prayer time should remind us to avoid selfishness and put the needs of others high on our prayer list.

Pray Regularly

In my years of ministry, the balance beam of my life has been to prioritize my time with God every morning before I get caught up in the duties and responsibilities of the day.

As you learn to pray regularly, your prayer life will become meaningful and joyful. Ignore any thoughts that tell you that taking time for prayer is impractical. Time spent in prayer is never wasted; it is invested.

Pray prepared to act as God reveals how you may become a part of the solution. Ask yourself:

- What influence has He given me for change?
- What resources are at my disposal?
- Who else shares my concern?

The best way to pray with regularity is to establish a daily, personal communion with God—a quiet time when you can be alone with Him. In this, you are following Christ's example as set in Mark 1:35. It is the only way to develop a close relationship with God. Time alone with Him sets a spiritual tone for the rest of your day—and make no mistake, you are engaged in a spiritual battle, so you need the strength and refreshment that come from spending time with God. Spiritual food cannot be "stored up," but unlimited spiritual resources are available to the person who spends time alone with God.

If you have not already made prayer a daily priority, choose a time when you are alert, such as early morning, and start meeting with God. Nineteenth-century missionary to China J. Hudson Taylor said, "Prayer in the morning is like tuning the orchestra before the symphony begins." The psalmist David said it well:

Listen to my voice in the morning, LORD. Each morning
I bring my requests to you and wait expectantly (Ps. 5:3).

To get the most out of your prayer time, choose a quiet place that is as private as possible and make this the place where you come to meet God on a daily basis. Avoid noise and distraction. Have your computer or paper and pen ready to write down intruding thoughts of "things to do." Allow unhindered time so that God can speak to your heart. Let Him speak through His Word, and occasionally, from hymns, devotional material and mental impressions as expressed in Philippians: "For God is working in you, giving you the desire and the power to do what pleases him" (Phil. 2:13). Use a variety of methods for your quiet time and vary the order. I suggest finding a quiet place with few visual distractions for those times when you really need to hear from God.

I want you to start doing something that may be hard for you to do: I want you to sit quietly before Him. Silent waiting to hear from God brings great reward. We live in an age of constant noise. Everyone seems to have something plugged into their ears. So try to wait for God in a room with no noise for at least one hour. You can work, read, sing; just no outside audible noise. Urban living makes this little experiment difficult, but please try it. After you've done it, recall what you thought about during that hour of silence. Did you find the quiet a bit unnerving? As you continue to wait on God, it will become a time of great renewal.

Spend Time Speaking to God

God hears your words. When you pray, aim for quality rather than quantity of time, and have as your objective meeting God, not preparing for a class you teach or a specific activity. Don't be mechanical or legalistic in your prayers. If you miss your quiet time, and it was your fault, confess it, thank God for His forgiveness and continue to walk in the Spirit. Do not be bound by guilt. A daily quiet time is not a good luck charm to make the day go right. Your greatest desire should be to spend as much time with God as possible because you love Him and want to be with Him.

Allow God to build this quiet time with Him as a regular discipline in your life. Ask God to make you continually hunger and thirst for Him. Ask Him to give you His wisdom on working out the details of your daily quiet time. He knows what is best for you individually.

When you come to meet God, come rested. Read a passage or two at bedtime and meditate on those words as you go to sleep. Periodically set aside an entire day for the sole purpose of seeking the Lord in prayer. Remember, some of that day will be spent just waiting and listening for what God is saying to you.

In biblical times, a garment of sackcloth was worn as a symbol of sincere penitence to God for national or personal sin. When covered with ashes, the rough and scratchy sackcloth accentuated an individual's distress and humiliation for sin. In addition to sackcloth and ashes, God commanded Old Testament believers to wear other symbolic reminders of spiritual truth. It troubles me that we have so many who profess to be "born again," yet little impact is being made on the spiritual life of our nation. Instead, the rampant philosophies are those that ignore or even deny God.

Yet, God shows us that without Him there is no foundation for man to be humane, but the greatest and most enduring happiness comes only through faith in Christ and His divine truths. God's mind and intentions can be changed through our prayer and repentance. Jonah prophesied doom to the wicked Assyrian city of Nineveh. As a result, the entire city repented in sackcloth and ashes (see Jonah 3:10). God will heal and renew our land, too, if only His people will humble themselves, pray for spiritual revival and change their ways concerning sin.

How to Pray Without Hindrance

There are no formulas for prayer, but there are scriptural principles that, if followed, will ensure that your prayers are effective. Look up the Scripture verses listed after each bullet point and linger on the words that the Holy Spirit is using to stir your heart.

- Resist the enemy (see Eph. 4:27; 6:11)
- Hide God's Word in your heart (see Ps. 119:11)
- Humble yourself before God (see 1 Pet. 5:6-10; Jas. 4:6)
- Maintain harmony in your relationships (see 1 Pet. 3:7-12)
- Abide in Christ and His Word (see John 15:7)
- Praise God—praise is your greatest defense against Satan. Claim Christ's authority over evil.

How to Pray with a Regular Partner

I have been blessed to have some precious prayer partners who pray for me daily. I may not know what they are praying or when they are praying, but I do know that they are covering me as I go about my day. Ask God to lead you to someone to be your prayer partner (men with men and women with women, or possibly a husband and wife team).

Plan a certain time, three or four times each week, to talk and pray over the phone. I suggest that with the prevalence of social networking, a voice-to-voice prayer is much more effective than reading something posted on the computer or phone. However, there is nothing wrong with sending prayerful thoughts to people. Keep a notebook or journal where you can write down prayer requests and answers that you and your prayer partner are praying for. Pray daily for your prayer partner. Develop an openness to share needs, not just general needs, but specific things. Spend time in prayer for these needs, problems or situations, and report back to each other answers to the prayers. The praise part of answered prayer is as important as the prayer.

When my dear husband, Bill, was in the final days of his life on this earth, his faith never wavered, and he was eager to encourage me every day to stay strong in my faith. During our years of ministry, I had prayed with many people, and we had witnessed God's intervention. I had every reason to be confident in my faith; however, when the love of your life and your partner in ministry is critically ill, the prayer support of family and friends is a great comfort. I feel certain that several people were praying for me on one particular day.

It was the first day the hospice workers were in our home with Bill. I had to go to the hair salon because I had a speaking engagement, and I felt confident with the level of care Bill would receive in my absence. At this stage in life, I was not driving long distances, but the hair salon was not far from our home and I most certainly could navigate my way. After a final check on Bill, I dashed to the car and proceeded to get onto the freeway.

Just up onto the freeway, my car began to chug-chug-chug. After I did a quick mental check of what might be wrong, the light flashing on the gas gauge presented a very clear picture of my predicament. Yes, I was out of gas. Fortunately, I managed to steer the car to the shoulder of the freeway, and there I sat. Remember, I had left the house in a hurry and was a bit overwhelmed by the presence of hospice workers in our home. My cell phone was not in my purse. I don't remember praying—maybe I did, maybe I didn't.

As I gazed through the windshield in disbelief, I saw a white van parked just a few yards ahead of me on the shoulder of the freeway. I got out of my car and approached the van. (Every time I get to this point in the story, someone moans at the thought of me getting out of my car and walking on the freeway.) As I peered in the van window I saw the female driver, and a small American flag perched on the dashboard. *Okay, this lady must be okay,* I thought. I quickly explained my dilemma and she offered me her cell phone.

I called home and spoke with Bill's assistant, Jason. Jason was calm as I explained what had happened. He did something so out of character for him . . . he suggested I ask the van driver to take me to the hair salon. He would make arrangements to get the car home and have someone pick me up. I had not told the lady driver my name, and she had not asked. She was driving a van with meals for shut-ins and was taking a break from her deliveries. She did have enough time to take me to the salon.

The moment I got into the van, my emotions gave way. I began to sob uncontrollably. The woman asked, "Do you believe in God?" I began to laugh. I explained that if the situation were reversed, I would have asked her the same question.

As we eased onto the freeway, I realized my life was in the hands of this total stranger. I don't remember praying . . . again . . . but maybe I did. Praying is such a part of my life that it was probably a subconscious reaction. I engaged the driver in conversation about her life and her work and she indicated that she was a believer. We pulled up to the salon and I slipped a $20 bill in her hand while she objected but smiled broadly. The driver and white van drove out of my life and she didn't know my name. As you have read this account, no doubt you have identified several points where I acted irresponsibly, beginning with not checking the gas gauge. Before you make a long list of my mistakes, let me take your attention to how good and gracious God was to me that day. So many people were praying for me. They knew I was dealing with the final days of Bill's life, and the emotional and physical toll was evident.

Remember how many times during that ordeal I had opportunities to pray, but I don't remember praying. There is a very profound truth about prayer found in this story. Prayer is the essence of my life, and not just words articulated and properly addressed to God my Father. Also, someone, somewhere, was praying for me. Oh how grateful I am for the prayers of others on my behalf! I do hope that if God brings someone to your mind, you will stop and pray.

Assignments for Creative Prayer

Although prayer should not be reduced to a formula, we have discovered over the years that it is helpful to include some basic elements in our communication with God: *Adoration, Confession, Thanksgiving, Supplication (ACTS)*.

A–Adoration

To adore God is to worship and praise Him, to honor and exalt Him in your heart and mind and with your lips. The Word of God teaches that your heavenly Father desires your fellowship, of which adoration is a vital part (see John 4:23-24; Heb. 12:28). Adoration expresses your complete trust in Him and reflects your confidence that He hears you. Adoration demonstrates your reverence, awe, love and gratitude.

C–Confession

When your discipline of prayer begins with adoration, the Holy Spirit has opportunity to reveal any sin in your life that needs to be confessed. By seeing God in His purity, His holiness, and His love, you become aware of your sinfulness and unworthiness. Confessing your sin and receiving His forgiveness restore you to fellowship with Him and clear the channel for God to hear and answer your prayers (see 1 John 1:7-9).

T–Thanksgiving

Nothing pleases God more than your consistent expression of faith. What better way to do this than to tell Him thank You? God's Word commands:

> Always be joyful. Keep on praying. No matter what happens, always be thankful, for this is God's will for you who belong to Christ Jesus (1 Thess. 5:16-18).

An attitude of thanksgiving enables you to recognize that God controls all things—not just the blessings, but the challenges and adversities as well. As you approach God with a thankful heart, He becomes strong on your behalf; conversely, a critical, unbelieving spirit displeases God and hinders His efforts to bless and enrich you and use you for His glory.

S–Supplication

Supplication includes petition for your own needs and intercession for others. We are to pray for everything and in specific terms.

As you talk to God, for example, pray that your inner person may be renewed, always sensitive to and empowered by the Holy Spirit. Pray about your problems, pray for wisdom and guidance, pray for strength to resist temptation, pray for comfort in time of sorrow—pray for everything.

Don't worry about anything; instead, pray about everything. Tell God what you need, and thank him for all he has done (Phil. 4:6).

Then pray for others—your spouse, your children, your parents, your neighbors and your friends. Pray for your pastor and missionaries and for various other Christians to whom God has given special responsibility. Pray for those in authority over you.

I urge you, first of all, to pray for all people. As you make your requests, plead for God's mercy upon them, and give thanks. Pray this way for kings and all others who are in authority, so that we can live in peace and quietness, in godliness and dignity (1 Tim. 2:1-2).

Pray especially for the salvation of souls, and for a daily opportunity to introduce others to Christ.

A Well-Rounded Prayer Life

These elements—Adoration, Confession, Thanksgiving, Supplication—have helped many Christians develop a more well-rounded prayer life.[4] Here are more suggestions to extend prayer into every area of life and your relationships with others, starting with your family:

1. Begin to develop habits of family prayer.

   • Take turns saying grace at mealtime.
   • As a husband and wife, take one or two minutes in the morning together to pray for each other's daily schedule.

- Pray for your children as they leave for school.
- Spend five minutes or more in family conversational prayer before the children go to bed.
- As a husband and wife, end the day praying together over family and personal concerns.

2. Practice intercessory prayer.

- Select one individual in a position of authority and/ or need and intercede for him or her every day for one week.
- Pray for one need from the front page of the newspaper, TV news report, or Internet alert each day.
- Pray for the conversion of influential individuals who by their attitudes and actions are known to be enemies of God. If they refuse to obey God, pray for their removal from positions of influence. I know some folks who print out pictures of various people and look at the image while they are praying.

3. Each week, research verses of Scripture to apply to one of the following:

- Those who are in authority
- People who do not know Christ
- Individuals who are ill
- Fellow believers
- Fulfillment of the Great Commission

4. Access information on prayer and listen to speakers who place an emphasis on prayer.

5. Read John 15.

- List the characteristics of a branch and how those characteristics apply in your life.
- List three specific prayer requests and pray, believing God for the answer.

6. Select a Scripture portion each day and pray through it in your quiet time.

7. Ask God for a prayer partner, someone with whom you can pray regularly about daily concerns.

Spend Time in Individual Worship and Prayer

Preparation

Begin your time with God early in the morning (see Ps. 5:3). Find a place where you can be alone, free from distractions. Take your Bible, a hymnbook, and notebook or your computer to record impressions from the Lord.

Enter his gates with thanksgiving; go into his courts with praise. Give thanks to him and bless his name (Ps. 100:4).

Ask God to search your heart (see Ps. 139:23-24). There is a vulnerability that comes when you are truly open to allow the Holy Spirit to convict you. I have shared frequently that early in my ministry I had many adjustments to make. Bill was so committed to do exactly what he believed God was calling him to do, and I desperately wanted to fit into that plan. Fortunately, the Spirit of the living God convicted me about my attitude, and after much prayer, I had a major attitude adjustment. Confess any sins the Holy Spirit reveals (see 1 John 1:9). At first I didn't see my attitude as sinful; however, when the Holy Spirit convicts, confession is the only option. Make certain you are walking and praying in the Spirit (see Eph. 5:15-20).

Wait on the Lord to worship Him (see Pss. 103; 104). I spoke with a young woman recently who has opened her home for one hour every day for friends and neighbors to come for a time of quiet meditation, prayer and praise. This is not an official prayer meeting. They come in and quietly sit and draw strength from being together, waiting on God. Unfortunately, in our modern culture we have shied away from meditation. To start, consider who God is and who Scripture reveals Him to be. Praise Him for His attributes. I have found it helpful to pray specifically regarding each one of the 13 attributes listed on the card my husband developed. I have listed those attributes in the Prayer Journal in the back of this book. Rejoice in your fellowship with Him, as He delights in you (see Prov. 15:8).

Read passages of Scripture and pray them back to God (see Pss. 146–150). Sing to the Lord, using your hymnbook, or sing along with recorded music, meditating upon and praying from the lyrics. When you sing, your attitude will change and your focus will turn from the challenges of the day.

Ask God to reveal the world to you from His point of view (see Isa. 55:8-9). Direct your thoughts away from material and physical needs toward eternal matters (see 2 Cor. 4:16-18).

If we get all of our information from media outlets about the events going on around the world, it is easy to become very discouraged. Asking God to give you perspective on world events will influence your prayers.

Intercession

Pray your way around the world with unhurried, detailed intercession for others. Begin with your non-Christian friends, relatives, neighbors, your pastor and church leadership, missionaries and other believers. Using news reports, continue on in prayer for your community, state and country. Pray for those in authority (see 1 Tim. 2:1-2) and any others God may bring to mind. Contact local officials and ask specific requests for them. You may be surprised how eager people are to give you prayer requests.

I recently received a letter from my friend Meredith in New York, reminding me of a very practical way to pray for a city that is easy to do and covers a large area of people:

> My husband, Ted, and I moved to New York City in 1976 for one year to work on the "I Found It" campaign. New York is so different from anywhere else—more people, more languages, more cultures. Would "I Found It" be effective here? Vonette was undaunted. She assembled the huge New York City phone books and tore out page after page. Wherever she traveled throughout the world in 1976 and early 1977, she handed out phone book pages and asked believers to pray for the listed New Yorkers by name.

> In June 1977, the campaign made a great impact in New York. More than 800 churches in the metro area participated, and nearly 18,000 New Yorkers indicated they had received

Christ. The momentum of the campaign spurred the growth of countless cooperative ministry efforts in the City, including a large and ongoing prayer ministry. Sociologist Tony Carnes points to the late 1970s as a turning point in Christian presence and influence in New York.[5]

For years afterward, I frequently met Christians who, when they found out I lived in New York, told me they had prayed in 1976–1977 for the Cruzes in the Bronx or the Valentinos in Brooklyn, or others throughout the metro area.

Meredith's letter continued:

> Today Campus Crusade for Christ has more than 70 staff representing 10 ministries in New York, an ongoing legacy of the prayer foundation laid by Vonette and the New York City phone books. And Ted and I are still here. In addition, I neglected to mention that the campaign was supported by a very active prayer chain: there were 15,496 believers who committed to pray for at least 15 minutes a day for "I Found It." Prayer works.

It is such a simple thing to do, yet, when I was prompted by the Holy Spirit to use the phone book, I don't remember worrying about what people would think. I just knew that focused, specific prayer could move the hand of God.

Pray as Paul prayed for others in Philippians 1, Colossians 1, and Ephesians 1 and 3. These chapters of Scripture reveal powerful intercession prayers that are useful in praying for yourself and others. Just change the pronouns for the occasion. You may want to choose one of Paul's prayers and pray it over your children through the years. Don't forget to ask for others what you ask for yourself. Desire for them what the Lord has shown you.

Personal Petition

Ask for understanding (see Ps. 119:18). Meditate on Scripture you have memorized or Scripture promises you know. Read an entire book in the Bible (select one of appropriate length). Ask God to show you personal applications. Pray for yourself. Ask, "Lord, what do You think of my life?" Consider your activities: What are your life and ministry objectives? How do you spend the majority of your time? Are your activities counting for eternity? Record your thoughts. Review or plan your use of time for God's greatest glory in various areas of your life: family, work, personal Bible study and devotions, and church activities. Discuss with the Lord problems or decisions you may be facing. My husband always reminded me that Christians don't have problems, just opportunities to see God work. Record conclusions God brings to your mind. Look in the Scriptures for promises to claim, and underline them.

We know that prayer is a tool of our spiritual warfare, but scientists are now concluding that prayer positively affects our minds and bodies.

> This powerful idea had not been addressed in much of the scientific literature, so Dr. Koenig decided to study it. His research started an academic trend, and Dr. Koenig is now the co-director of the Center for Spirituality, Theology and Health at Duke University Medical Center—a juxtaposition of science and theology that would have been hard to imagine three decades ago. . . .
>
> On top of that, people who attend religious services are almost 50 percent less likely to have high interlueken-6 levels (which indicate poor immune system function) than are people who don't attend services.

In plain English, the more religious you are, the less stressed out you tend to be. Which often means you're healthier. . . .

And the doctors who are out on the front lines seem to agree: According to a 2007 survey published in the *Archives of Internal Medicine,* 54 percent of doctors said "a supernatural being" (aka God) sometimes affects a patient's health."[6]

The article was quite lengthy; however, the conclusion was the most profound: In other words, in this crazy world of difficulty and heartache, in this scary economy, in these hard times, you *do* have a prayer.

Science seems to be catching up with what believers have long known!

The great scientist Sir Isaac Newton said, "I can take my telescope and look millions and millions of miles into space, but I can lay it aside and go into my room, shut the door, get down on my knees in earnest prayer, and see more of heaven and get closer to God than I can assisted by all the telescopes and material agencies on earth."

Notes

1. George Washington's personal prayer, cited in W. Herbert Burk, B.D., *Washington's Prayers* (Norristown, PA: Published for the benefit of the Washington Memorial Chapel, 1907), pp. 87-95.
2. Joseph Kenneth Grider, *Baker's Dictionary of Theology* (Grand Rapids, MI: Baker Books, 1960).
3. S. D. Gordon, *Quiet Talks on Prayer* (Charleston, SC: BiblioBazaar, 2007), p. 11.
4. Bill Bright, *The Christian and Prayer* (Orlando, FL: New Life Publications, 1994).
5. Tony Carnes, cited in Anna Karpathakis, *New York Glory* (New York: NYU Press, 2001).
6. Katharine Whittemore, "Let Us Pray," *Ladies Home Journal,* July 10, 2010.

Chapter 4

The Dynamics of Group Prayer

In chapter 3, I said that so many people just don't know how to pray. You have an opportunity to change that in your life and in the lives of others. If God is nudging you to join a prayer group, or perhaps leading you to form a prayer group, you can experience the blessings that are in store for all those who make group prayer a priority: Participants will learn how to experience an exciting prayer life of intercession. Timid individuals will discover the blessings of praying aloud without self-consciousness. Prayer group members will experience many answers to prayer as they learn to pray together in one accord. Bonds of fellowship will grow strong as individuals share common concerns in prayer. Participants will become more creative in prayer as they support each other in prayer and learn to pray together.

Guidelines for Group Prayer

Praying aloud is difficult for some people. Children will be frank to say, "I don't like to pray aloud" or "Why should I pray?" or "I don't know what to say." On the other hand, many adults feel the need to pray but hesitate to come to a meeting where there will be prayer because they feel like the children but are afraid to admit it. Only God has the answers to the troubles that are on every mind, and He has instructed us to come to Him as little children in prayer.

Encourage each other in your prayer group to be honest in prayer. Say "I" when you mean "I"; say "we" when you mean "we." Talk things over with God as with a friend. Include expressions of love and adoration such as "I love You, Lord." Pray aloud when you are alone so that you can become accustomed to hearing the sound of your voice in prayer. Write out your prayers once in a while and bring them to read aloud in the prayer group during the time of prayer. This will accustom you to hearing your voice praying in a group.

I have some suggestions for conducting an initial spontaneous prayer session.

Divide the participants into groups of four to six people. Make sure the group members have met and you have allowed a brief time to get acquainted. Ask the individuals to briefly share a prayer from the past that they remember most. Guide the prayer time, instructing everyone by saying:

- Verbalize a short, simple prayer in six words or so.

- Talk to God as you would to a friend present in the group. Conversational prayer is the expression of the human heart in conversation with God.

- Speak in modern conversational language. The more natural your prayer, the more real God becomes to you.

- Avoid making a "prayer speech" or "preaching" at others during prayer.

- Pray as often as you wish, but don't monopolize the time. It is not necessary to pray around the circle.

- Experienced pray-ers, keep your prayers short and simple. You may struggle to simplify your words as much as the beginner struggles to verbalize. But doing this will enhance rapport and help prevent the shy individual from being intimidated.

- The person who has never prayed aloud before will feel more comfortable joining in when experienced Christians are praying simple sentences as the beginners do.

- Mature Christians often have difficulty in praying aloud or praying meaningful personal prayers.

- With this method, everyone will feel more comfortable in beginning to pray aloud, for no one can tell who is experienced and who is the beginner.

Direct participants in conversational prayer by introducing the following ideas one at a time:

- Say thank you for one thing, e.g., the Lord Jesus, God's love, His forgiveness, the beautiful day, and so on.

- Say thank you for something that has happened in your life in the last 24 hours.

- Use "Please help . . ." (yourself or someone else) sentences.

- Ask for one thing for yourself.

Thank God for how He will meet those desires and requests. Continue praying spontaneously, introducing requests during prayer and allowing an opportunity to pray back and forth on a single request or subject until everyone who wants to participate seems finished.

Let everyone pray as the Spirit directs. There is always the risk that someone will dominate the time. You may have to interrupt if this happens. Don't be concerned about silence—God speaks in silence. Let God speak to you. Use the time to pray for things you would not want to voice before others. Close with a final prayer of thanksgiving, acknowledging God's faithfulness, love and sovereignty.

Spontaneous prayer sessions need variety. You can select various Scripture passages or devotional materials and read portions that will prompt a responsive prayer. Ask individuals to share a favorite Scripture passage and discuss how that passage would encourage them to pray. Refer to and claim specific verses of Scripture for particular requests.

Encourage individuals to pray continually. You will find that the more you structure specific times of prayer, the more you will realize that it is possible to continually be in prayer. Remind group members that God commands us to pray without ceasing (see 1 Thess. 5:17). *Never stop praying.*

Encourage them to recognize that God is present wherever they go and that He is always ready to answer prayer. Talk about how important it is to thank God for everything He allows into our lives—everything from a beautiful day to a flat tire. When we learn to thank God for the simple everyday events of life, then when times of crisis come, we will find it more natural to thank God for His faithfulness and trust Him through the crisis. Encourage your prayer group members to talk to God when they feel a need—any time of the day or night.

Suggest that they use their time twice by developing a habit of praying as they go about daily activities that do not require total concentration—for example, while showering, driving, gardening, doing tasks with their hands in which their minds are free.

Instruct individuals to concentrate on what another person is praying, agreeing in their hearts. We are instructed to pray in one accord. Trust the Holy Spirit to direct your thoughts and prayer when it is your turn to pray. Do not be thinking ahead to what you will pray—you will miss the other person's prayer and neglect to pray in one accord.

Emphasize that the Early Church was accused of turning the world upside down when they practiced praying in one accord (see Acts 4:24-31).

Read about how an earthquake opened prison doors for Paul and Silas when they prayed together (see Acts 16:25-26).

And most of all, remember that Jesus Christ is actually present in the room.

> I tell you this: Whatever you prohibit on earth is prohibited in heaven, and whatever you allow on earth will be allowed in heaven. "I also tell you this: If two of you agree down here on earth concerning anything you ask, my Father in heaven will do it for you. For where two or three gather together because they are mine, I am there among them" (Matt. 18:18-20).

Stimulate Intercessory Prayer

The Bible gives us examples of men and women of faith who saw God answer intercessory prayer in a mighty way. In Genesis 18–19, we read the account of Abraham pleading with God to save the city of Sodom. The conversation that Abraham had with God has always been an encouragement to me to ask God, then listen to see if the Holy Spirit impresses me to alter my request. Abraham changed his prayer several times. So encourage people to listen as well as ask in the intercessory process.

When Abraham prayed, Lot was saved (see Gen. 19:29). When Hezekiah prayed, God turned back Sennacherib (see 2 Kings 19). Jesus healed people in response to intercession:

- Mark 2:3-5: Four friends brought the paralytic before Jesus.
- Matthew 15:22-28: A Canaanite woman came to Jesus on behalf of her daughter.
- Matthew 17:15-21: A man sought healing for his son.

An angel set Peter free in response to united prayer. The Early Church flourished as Paul interceded for them (see Rom. 1:9).

The earnest prayer of a righteous man has great power and wonderful results. In James 5:17-18, we read, "Elijah was as human as we are, and yet when he prayed earnestly that no rain would fall, none fell for three and a half years! Then he prayed for rain, and down it poured. The grass turned green, and the crops began to grow again."

Emphasize the priority God places on praying for those in authority (see 1 Tim. 2:1-4).

Encourage individuals to make notes of the intercessory prayers of Jesus, Paul and Peter during their personal Bible study and pattern their own prayers along similar lines.

Pray through Scripture portions to intercede for others, letting the Scripture guide your prayers and express your thoughts to God. Here are some examples:

- Pray for a member of your family (see Eph. 1:16-19).
- Pray for your Sunday School teacher (see Eph. 3:14-16).
- Pray for a Christian friend (see Phil. 1:9-11).
- Pray for your pastor (see Col. 1:9-11).

To establish a pastor-people prayer team, enlist volunteers to pray one day a month for their pastor. Sign up members from the congregation, designating specific days of the month they will pray.

Ask the pastor to share his weekly or daily prayer requests. These individuals may covenant to pray as they go about their daily tasks or take time from work for prayer and fasting. The individuals designated to pray each week may even choose to be on their knees, praying in another room while the pastor is speaking in the pulpit on Sundays.

Organize a group of women to pray in the same manner for the pastor's wife.

Practice Intercessory Prayer in a Group

Prepare prayer requests on slips of paper to be given out ahead of time. Select prayer requests from:

- Community events or concerns
- Local elected officials
- Shared email requests
- Personal urgent needs

Pass out prayer requests at each session. Make the requests specific rather than general. Pray in one accord, remembering common concerns and allowing each participant an opportunity to pray for each subject before introducing a new subject.

Make your prayers specific in order that specific answers may be recognized as they come. Assign someone to record specific requests when they are first introduced. Pray together concerning international problems, the leaders of your nation, the concerns of your community, your church, your pastor, the needs in your home and family—but remember to pray in faith. God answers the prayer of faith. Feel free to add additional requests as they come to mind.

Record God's answers as they become apparent. Share with the group reports of answered prayer.

Pray for the Fulfillment of the Great Commission

You can win men and women to Christ through prayer. Pray that God would prepare the heart to understand and respond to the gospel (see John 6:44).

Pray that God would raise up a believer to share the gospel with the unbeliever (see Matt. 9:37).

Recognize that Satan has blinded and captivated the unbeliever, and acknowledge Christ's victory over him (see Eph. 6:12).

Persist in these prayers (see Dan. 10:12).

Build up believers in Christ through prayer. Thank God for them. Pray for deliverance from evil companions (see 2 Thess. 3:2). Pray that they might walk worthy of the Lord (see Col. 1:10). Pray for wisdom and revelation in the knowledge of Christ (see Eph. 1:16). Pray for them to be strengthened with might by His Spirit in the inner man (see Eph. 3:14). Pray for their unity in the spirit with other believers (see John 17:23). Pray that their love may abound and that they may approve things that are excellent (see Phil. 1:9).

Pray for boldness and opportunities to share the gospel (see Col. 4:3). Pray that they may be completely mature and be fully assured in all the will of God (see Col. 4:12). Persist in these prayers.

Send out laborers through prayer. Recognize the problem of the labor shortage (see Matt. 9:37). Make a list of candidates to be sent by the Lord (see Isa. 6:8) and pray persistently for them. Pray that laborers would be thrust forth into specific communities and countries. Claim the fulfillment of the Great Commission in your area and the whole world according to His command and promise (see Matt. 28:18-20).

Guidelines for Forming and Maintaining Prayer Groups

Individuals from many different backgrounds will come together to form a prayer group and grow in their relationship with God. As individuals learn to focus on Jesus Christ and unite in prayer for common concerns, denominational differences diminish in importance. God works through united prayer to change lives and alter circumstances.

Even in this age of electronic communication and social networking, there is no substitute for meeting with a group of people committed to pray. There is so much strength and power in the group dynamic.

How to Host a Prayer Group

Give prayer a priority in your own life. Ask God for a co-leader, if you like, to assist in delivering invitations and leading the meetings. Prepare to teach a group how to pray after studying the materials presented earlier in this book.

Invite individuals in your sphere of influence who could be available to meet to pray—neighbors on your street, students in your dorm, employees where you work, others God brings to mind.

Make personal contact with each individual. Pray for each one, that God would prepare their hearts to be involved in a prayer group. Individuals who have never received Jesus Christ as their Savior may, and should, be invited. Many people have been reached for Christ by attending prayer groups. Deliver to each person a personal invitation. Follow up the initial invitation. Invite Christian friends from your church and other areas. Perhaps they will desire to form additional prayer groups. Plan an informal gathering. Invite about three times as many as you want to come and trust God for the participants He wishes to bring. Limit each prayer group to approximately 20. If more attend, divide into two or more groups. The number of participants in a prayer group may be as small as two.

Select and Prepare a Place to Meet

As you've read my comments, you may think I am stating the obvious. But you will be surprised how many people will respond positively to a prayer meeting if you have made proper arrangements.

Select an appropriate location to meet regularly. This may be your home, at your church, at an office, a meeting room in a restaurant, or a site off campus. Choose a spot where participants can sit facing one another. It is imperative to be free of interruptions. Request that cell phones be turned off.

Prepare for the arrival of participants. On the day of the meeting, you may wish to post a sign, as a reminder, saying, "Prayer Meeting Here Today." Be creative. Provide nametags each time until participants become well acquainted. Prepare slips to hand out containing prayer requests from national and local leaders.

Conduct an Introductory Prayer Meeting

Welcome each guest warmly as he or she arrives. Any time you bring a group together, the first meeting can make some feel anxious because they don't know exactly what is going to happen.

Nametags can be helpful if your group has people who do not know each other. Offer simple refreshments, if appropriate and you desire to serve something to eat or drink. This is not necessary, but it helps guests relax. Begin getting acquainted by asking everyone to take one to two minutes to share the following personal information:

- Facts they like to share with others, such as where they were born, where they live, what they do, details about their family, and special interests or hobbies.
- What they desire to gain from the prayer meetings.

After about 20 minutes, ask God's blessing and guidance and proceed with the meeting.

Hand each person the prayer reminder card. Give individuals an opportunity to submit personal prayer requests. Ask them to state their request in one or two brief sentences. Remind them that the Lord knows all the details of their needs and that you have met to spend time in prayer bringing requests before the Lord. Express your enthusiasm for prayer and your desire to learn and grow as you all meet and pray together. Explain that you will begin by using guidelines from this book and that you will all be learning together. Lead the group in spontaneous prayer.

Remember to pray for the requests handed out and those voiced earlier. Allow time for unhurried prayer. End the prayer time when you have covered all the requests or at least five minutes before the time to close, thanking God for the privilege of bringing these requests to Him. Encourage guests to use their prayer reminder card every day, praying for a request each day as the Holy Spirit brings it to mind.

Suggest they practice praying aloud when alone and, if they wish, write out a prayer to bring the next time you meet as a group. Confirm the time and place for the next meeting.

How to Conduct the Second Prayer Meeting

Open with prayer and a brief time of sharing answers to last week's prayers. Read aloud together a selected memory verse. Spend the remaining time in spontaneous group prayer. Lead in prayer, setting an example with short, simple prayers of praise and thanksgiving as in the first session. Suggest that individuals introduce prayer requests during the prayer time and that others pray in agreement. Use the prayer reminder cards and other requests handed out the week before. Encourage participants to read aloud the prayer they brought with them if they chose to write out a prayer. End the prayer time five minutes before time to close.

Assign a memory verse for the following week from the list. Acknowledge that there may be those present who are unsure of their relationship with God. Invite anyone who wants to be sure of his or her relationship with God to remain afterwards for a few minutes. Explain the contents of the booklet "How to Know God Personally" (see appendix B). Give the individual the opportunity to pray to receive Christ.

How to Structure Future Prayer Meetings

Modify the format of a group prayer meeting to fit your individual situation; however, the following elements should be included:

- An opening prayer
- A brief time of sharing answered prayer

- A group review of the previous week's memory verse (optional)
- Inspiration and/or instruction
- Interaction

Offer participants an opportunity to submit personal prayer requests. Avoid lengthy discussions; this is a time to focus on prayer. Encourage those with problems to seek solutions from Scripture and believe God for answered prayer. If someone tends to monopolize the sharing time, politely ask someone else for prayer requests. Be sensitive to the spiritual needs of those who participate. Be available to share with those who are not Christians or who are defeated Christians. For those who are not Christians, explain the content of the booklet "How to Know God Personally" (see appendix B). For defeated Christians, explain the ministry of the Holy Spirit as it is explained in the booklet "Satisfied" (see appendix D).

Avoid discussions of a controversial, doctrinal or personal nature. Allow an unhurried time for spontaneous group prayer. Allot approximately one-half to three-quarters of the total time to actual prayer. Include an up-to-date record and report of prayer requests and answers. This stimulates interest and increases faith. Assign a memory verse containing praise or a promise. Begin and end on time. Encourage all members of the prayer group to invite their friends to subsequent meetings.

How to Sustain Interest Among Participants

Encourage members to attend regularly. If participants miss a meeting without contacting you, call to say "We missed you. Are you okay?"

Let them know you value their contribution to the group. Delegate the contacting of absent group members to different participants.

Communicate enthusiasm in making requests and sharing answers. Pray for issues of mutually vital interest to participants. Direct prayers toward specific requests in order that participants may see specific answers. Teach and review the material in this book. Follow different prayer patterns. Rotate assignments for five-minute devotionals among participants. Review and discuss books and articles on prayer.

Plan activities to motivate prayer. Here are some ideas: Plan a day of prayer or an overnight prayer retreat in special surroundings; invite an inspirational speaker to speak during your prayer time; plan periodic social gatherings for families or close friends of participants; get the group together just for fun times; team up prayer partners for a specified period of time to telephone or meet regularly for prayer. Consider switching periodically. Structure an emergency telephone/email prayer chain. Covenant to pray daily for short-term emergency concerns.

You might think about combining with other prayer groups for special events such as workshops, retreats, days of prayer, rallies, coffees or meals. Choose a common project about which you commit your time, talent and/or treasure, such as regular evangelistic outreach, days of witnessing, support of an orphan or missionary work. Listen as a group to messages on prayer.

How to Build Personal Relationships with Group Members

Pray for each person in your group as the Holy Spirit brings them to mind. Take time to become acquainted with individual participants. Take the initiative according to your personality and time schedule. The following are some suggestions.

You can develop spiritually together by studying the Bible as a group or reading through the Bible in one year together. Pray about each other's needs and concerns. Memorize Scripture together. Send notes or surprises that arrive in the mail. Remember birthdays and take advantage of other holidays to send greetings. Show special kindnesses. Visit a group member who is sick, under pressure or working hard. Take cookies or a small remembrance. Don't stay long, simply let him or her know that you care.

Maintain contact via phone, email, text to let them know they are on your mind and are important to you. Don't always have a specific reason or request in mind. Phone just to say hi. This takes a little time but demonstrates thoughtfulness. To avoid prolonged conversations, explain in the beginning that you are limited to a certain number of minutes for your conversation. Spend time doing things together—shopping, attending sporting or other events—to get better acquainted.

Chapter 5

Prayer in the Church

Something new and special takes place in a body of believers who learn to pray in one accord. A strong prayer base increases unity and excitement among all who participate. As God answers united prayer, both faith and ministries grow.

Unfortunately, much of the church is asleep. The mindset of many is a sense of security. We as the church of the Living God must awaken to the power of prayer.

I know there are churches with very effective prayer ministries, and I am not suggesting that you ever try to undo any existing prayer emphasis. However, there are many opportunities to improve what is being done in the local church. I can't imagine any pastor objecting to someone wanting to coordinate prayer activities.

This chapter contains suggestions on how to introduce a strong prayer emphasis in the local church. It is offered primarily as resource material for the pastor or someone he may wish to delegate as a prayer coordinator within the church. It would also be useful for any other individual who has a vision for initiating a prayer movement in a Christian group or organization.

To initiate a prayer movement for evangelizing your community and discipling believers, you must first recognize the local church as God's primary instrument for evangelizing communities and discipling believers. These are the purposes of the church:

- To reach every non-Christian in the community with the good news of Jesus Christ
- To make mature, witnessing disciples of all its members
- To glorify Christ by serving the community

Prayer is the key to seeing God work in the lives of individuals, whole churches, cities, nations and the world. So make prayer a vital part of your church movement of evangelism and discipleship.

Ask God to begin a prayer movement in your church. This is necessary if the church is truly going to see its purpose of evangelism and discipleship fulfilled. Dr. Vernon Grounds said, "The average layman prays less than five minutes a day."

Envision in your mind's eye what can happen in a local church where a prayer movement is taking place. Ask yourself: *What happened in the Early Church? What is happening in other churches? What can happen in my church?*

When you initiate a movement of prayer in your church, you are not just successfully developing a program of prayer. A prayer movement will bring life change in the participants as well as the entire church body.

How to Establish a Prayer Movement with the Local Church
Give prayer priority in the church.

I will bring them also to my holy mountain of Jerusalem and will fill them with joy in my house of prayer (Isa. 56:7).

Jesus said in Mark 11:17, "The Scriptures declare, 'My Temple will be called a house of prayer for all nations,' but you have turned it into a den of thieves."

The church is not called a house of evangelism or a house of worship or a house for social gatherings. Pray that your pastor and church staff will have a vision for the involvement of their members in a city prayer ministry. The role of church leaders is made clear in Ephesians:

> He is the one who gave these gifts to the church: the apostles, the prophets, the evangelists, and the pastors and teachers. Their responsibility is to equip God's people to do his work and build up the church, the body of Christ, until we come to such unity in our faith and knowledge of God's Son that we will be mature and full grown in the Lord, measuring up to the full stature of Christ (Eph. 4:11-13).

It is my prayer that every pastor set the example by his personal prayer life, leadership and involvement. Ideally, a prayer ministry in the local church would be given the same level of influence as other ministries, such as youth, adults, men, women, music.

Challenge a potential prayer leadership group to commit themselves to training and personal involvement in prayer as a priority. Begin with a group that will provide the overall leadership for developing an ongoing prayer movement. The criteria for selecting this leadership group should include trained members who have:

- A vision for reaching the community through prayer
- Proven leadership potential
- Effective personal prayer lives
- A schedule that is not already heavily burdened with responsibility

Use the material in this book and the many other valuable resources available on prayer.

Ask permission of your church's leadership to teach a class on "How to Pray Effectively."

The class should include the following topics:

- Evaluating your relationship with God and preparing to enter His presence
- Hindrances to your prayer life
- Appropriating the filling of the Holy Spirit
- Basic principles of prayer
- Departing to a lonely place to pray
- The power of prayer
- The priority of prayer
- Intercessory prayer

Teach people to pray claiming specific verses of Scripture (see Ps. 51:1-2; Dan. 4:34-37; Heb. 6:18). Introduce what it means to pray through the Scriptures (you can use Paul's prayers in his epistles, for a start). Introduce and practice spontaneous prayer. Allow time in each class for individuals to share recent specific answers to prayer. Give prayer assignments each week. Suggest that everyone choose a prayer partner—someone with whom to pray frequently and regularly about personal and general concerns.

Challenge people with historical biblical passages indicating God's intervention in times of crises (see the bulleted list that follows). Demonstrate, using Scripture, how throughout history there have been various crises that have threatened the well-being of a nation and demanded specific, united prayer.

Explain that without exception, when people united in specific prayer, God heard, answered, provided, delivered, empowered, conquered—whatever was needed. Here are some examples:

- God warns the people of Judah about their lack of concern, decadence and immorality (see Ezek. 8-9).

- God promises to hear and answer the humble prayer of His people (see 2 Chron. 7:14).

- The men of Judah cried to the Lord and He routed their enemy (see 1 Chron. 12:1-20).

- Troubled Judah follows Israel's example in turning back to the Lord, and He gives them rest on all sides (see 2 Chron. 15:1-9).

- While Judah praises the Lord, the attacking enemies destroy each other (see 2 Chron. 20:1-23).

- Judah's leadership does wrong, does not repent and is defeated by a small army (see 2 Chron. 24:15-27).

- Hezekiah leads Judah and Israel back to seeking the Lord (see 2 Chron. 29:1-30).

- The people weep in repentance upon hearing the Word of God after being removed from it for years (see Neh. 8).

- Leaders humble themselves and pray to seek and receive God's protection (see Ezra 8:21-23).

- Persecuted believers ask for and receive boldness and abundant grace as they unite in one heart and mind in specific prayer (see Acts 4:1-35).

- The people pray that Esther will receive favor before the king, and their prayer is answered (see Esther 4:16).

In each case, united prayer brought dramatic, powerful intervention by God on their behalf. Explain how Jonah 3 is an example of the fulfillment of the promise of God in 2 Chronicles 7:14.

Review the passages in the book of Joel that explain how, in the face of a critical national emergency, God's people are called three times to united prayer (see Joel 1:1-20; 2:1-32; 3:1-21). Share how the Spirit of God stirs Christians to pray in great numbers.

For example, the great American revival of 1857–1858 was born in prayer. A businessman layman, Jeremiah Lanphier, was burdened by the conditions of downtown New York and was employed by the Dutch Reformed denomination as a city missionary. He called a prayer meeting on July 1, 1857, which was attended by six people. The second week, 20 came, then 40. Soon they decided to meet daily. The prayer meeting was so popular that other churches had to open their doors for noontime prayer. Within six months, 10,000 people were praying daily for revival. Revival swept across the country.

Emphasize that 1 Timothy 2:1-4 lays a responsibility upon Christians to meet together to pray for all those in authority.

Appoint a prayer coordinator in the church, a pastor or a lay husband-and-wife team.

Choose six couples, each of whom will assume one of the following responsibilities:

- **Organize small prayer groups and direct new people into each of these groups.** Teach workshops for new people as they enter the prayer movement. Prepare monthly praise and prayer sheets. Plan prayer events such as nights of watching, days of prayer and fasting, and so on. Pair and follow up prayer partners and pastor-people prayer teams counseling individuals in prayer.

- **Plan specific prayer involvement.** Harness the enthusiasm and potential of the training with an effective ongoing prayer outreach within your church and in the community.

- **Plan a citywide prayer workshop** in cooperation with other churches and/or the city coordinator. Initiate or participate in a city, national and world united prayer strategy.

- **Sponsor a prayer rally.** Prayer rallies have proven to be a source of great encouragement to those who participate. There is evidence of long-lasting results from prayer rallies.

- **Establish a Prayer Task Force** in cooperation with local National Prayer committees.

- **Lead a Bible study** using the resources suggested in this book.

- **Establish a Sunday School class** for the specific and sole purpose of in-depth study of prayer for those who may be called to a ministry of prayer

How to Encourage Spontaneous Small-Group Prayer in Your Congregation

Explain how the church can have an influence on the city and the world right where you are through prayer.

Divide into small groups of 4 to 6 people.

Put different people in a group each week.

Mix or divide by interests or age groups.

Distribute prayer request lists prepared from the needs of your church, individuals, city, nation and world. When requests become too numerous, divide the lists, giving a different portion to each group. Pray through the requests. Be sure to report answers.

Divide the congregation into family groups for prayer, encouragement and concern. Most churches have cell groups or home groups; however, many are not family groups. It is vitally important to have families praying with other families.

How to Reach the Community for Christ Through Prayer
Select members of the prayer leadership group and qualified volunteers who have been trained. Challenge them to do the following:

- Teach prayer training classes.
- Form prayer groups in their homes, offices, at school or other areas of individual influence.
- Be alert for opportunities for evangelism as individuals learn how to pray and begin to receive answers.

Recruit others to encourage individuals or coordinate and administrate individual and church-wide prayer requests and needs. Establish a 24-hour prayer chain in your church or city. Pray for homes and individuals being contacted by evangelism teams. Collect and prepare citywide prayer requests.

How to Unite the City Churches in Prayer
Contact pastors throughout your city. Communicate your vision for helping to reach the city for Christ through prayer. Offer to help coordinate training of their laymen in prayer. Ask them to appoint a prayer coordinator in their church. Work with church coordinators to plan workshops and prayer training sessions in individual churches. Offer your prayer leadership group as trainers and coordinators with other churches.

Unite the interested churches of a city in prayer by sharing requests.

Saturate the city with prayer groups by encouraging each church to implement the prayer plan.

Cooperate and encourage other churches to unite in a strategy for neighborhood prayer groups in your city.

Reach the World Through Prayer

You can encourage your church to become a model in prayer for other churches by challenging members to pray for the nation and the world toward the fulfillment of the Great Commission.

I want to share with you material developed by Dick Eastman.[1] Dick is the international president of Every Home for Christ. In his role, he has traveled around the world more than 40 times to every continent. I believe you will benefit greatly if you use the pattern for prayer that Dick has described.

Every Tribe

By looking at the end result of a fully evangelized world, as described in Revelation 5:8-10, we discover an interesting four-fold focus for systematic prayer.

And when he took the scroll, the four living beings and the twenty-four elders fell down before the Lamb. Each one had a harp, and they held gold bowls filled with incense—the prayers of God's people! And they sang a new song with these words: "You are worthy to take the scroll and break its seals and open it. For you were killed, and your blood has ransomed people for God from every tribe and language and people and nation. And you have caused them to become God's Kingdom and his priests. And they will reign on the earth" (Rev. 5:8-10).

Because a "tribe" is not a full nation, we may conclude that this word is a reference to smaller groups within a nation, such as "cultural groups."

"Culture" means "the totality of socially transmitted behavior or patterns, arts, beliefs, institutions, and all other products of human work and thought characteristic of a community or population." Some ethnic groups within a nation have clearly defined patterns of behavior or beliefs that differ greatly from the general beliefs of the nation in which the group exists.

Because there are several worldwide ministries that specifically target "hidden people groups," the kindred objective provides us with the following prayer focus: *frontier evangelism.* We need to pray for all ministries laboring to evangelize hidden peoples.

Every Language

According to Scripture, at the final judgment converts will come from all languages of the earth, a clear indication that the gospel will have been given to all these people. Our prayers are important for this second focus: *translation evangelism,* which is accomplished by ministries working in Bible translation in order that every language group can be evangelized.

Every People

The word "people" in the Greek (*laos*) appears 143 times in the New Testament and refers to "human beings." The emphasis is upon the individual. Whole nations are not evangelized until people are evangelized, one at a time. Especially important to evangelizing people of a given nation is to reach them with a message that they can comprehend in the context of their own culture. For this reason, our third prayer focus is *national evan-*

gelism, or evangelistic programs developed and presented by nationals who actually live in that nation.

Every Nation

Appearing 164 times in the New Testament, the word "nation" (from the Greek *ethnos*) is most commonly translated "Gentiles." It refers to the nations of the world other than Israel. Some mission leaders believe it is another reference to the multiplied thousands of hidden people groups. I believe it also refers to the total population of people living within geographic boundaries at any given time. Thus, our final focus includes *systematic evangelism*. Systematic evangelism is attempted by ministries that seek to organize Christian nationals to systematically reach all the people of their nation with the gospel.[2]

Practical Application for Teaching on Prayer

Prayer changes things. Throughout history, men and women of faith have seen God as bigger than themselves—all-powerful and willing to hear and answer prayer. They knew that prayer is the key to releasing God's power—the only way, ultimately, to change the world.

Today, we are those men and women. In these times of crisis, of rampant crime, of the disintegration of the family, of economic disaster, of moral and spiritual bankruptcy . . . we must pray. But how? What do we say? How do we communicate with the God of the universe who wants us to know Him as our Father?

Why is training in prayer so important? "Call to Me," God offers. "And I will answer you," He promises (see Ps. 86:7). I continue to discover that men and women would respond to this command if they knew how to pray specifically and with authority. We've also found that through simple training, the dynamics of effective prayer can become the most exciting part of any believer's experience.

Prayer Patterns to Employ

I have already alluded to these patterns of prayer throughout the book, but I want to list them here in one section for your easy access. I have used the following prayer patterns in many seminars during my years of ministry, and over and over again participants will comment that these practical steps have given them a prayer life with meaning. The prayer patterns may be used individually or with a group.

A. Pray in modern language, in six words or less:

   1. "Thank you" for one thing, such as the Lord Jesus, the beautiful day and so on
   2. "Thank you" for something that has happened in your life in the past 24 hours
   3. "Please help. . ." (yourself or someone else)
   4. Ask for one thing for yourself
   5. Thank God for how He will meet those desires and requests

B. Choose a psalm (for example, Pss. 103; 145–150) or another passage of praise Scripture to pray back to God.

C. Choose a specific Scripture related to a particular need:

   1. Salvation
   2. Illness

D. Areas of Influence:

1. Government
2. The Home and Family
3. The Church
4. News and Education Media
5. Entertainment Media
6. Education
7. Judicial System
8. Business and Commerce
9. Medical Service

E. Elements of Prayer:

1. Adoration—Recognize God's attributes, His nature
2. Waiting—Develop a holy stillness in God's presence
3. Confession—"Temple cleansing time"
4. Scripture—Word-enriched prayer
5. Watching—Develop a holy alertness
6. Intercession—Pray for others
7. Petition—Personal needs
8. Thanksgiving—Blessings and trials
9. Singing—Worship in song
10. Meditation—Mentally evaluate or ponder spiritual themes
11. Listen—Receive spiritual instruction
12. Praise—Begin and end with worshiping God

Spend five minutes on each point.

F. Pray the names of God:

1. Jehovah-Jireh: God our provider
2. Jehovah-Rophe: God our healer

---

3. Jehovah-Nissi:	God our banner of victory
4. Jehovah-M'Kaddesh:	God our sanctification
5. Jehovah-Shalom:	God our peace
6. Jehovah-Rohi:	God our shepherd
7. Jehovah-Tsidkenu:	God our righteousness
8. Jehovah-Shammah:	God the ever-present one

I realize that you have a lot of material to digest. I really don't expect you to implement everything at one time; however, if you will make yourself available and seek God for His guidance, I know your prayers will be effective and your efforts will bear much fruit.

As I have prepared this book, my heart's desire is that many people will be open to making prayer the focus of their ministry. My husband always reminded people that God is not looking for ability but for availability. Please, dear one, be available for God to use you to pray and to encourage others to pray.

Notes

1. This material was first used in a publication for Campus Crusade for Christ and later in Vonette Bright and Ben A. Jennings, *Unleashing the Power of Prayer* (Chicago: Moody Press, 1989).
2. Ibid., p. 283.

Prayer
Journal

INTRODUCTION

The pages that follow make up a very practical prayer journal. I have received countless testimonies from people who have used this journal and found that it made a tremendous impact on their prayer life. I plead with you to make a commitment to use the journal for at least 30 days.

The first page for each day indicates the general topic for the day. Read the attribute of God and open your heart to receive God's leading for your prayer time. The better you understand the character of God, the greater your passion for prayer on each suggested topic. Add Scripture references as God reveals them to you and adjust the subjects as God leads.

The suggested daily subjects may occupy only a few seconds of your prayer time, or you may wish to concentrate on one issue, person or event for an extended time. The important point to remember is to name your specific request and to unite in prayer for designated subjects.

You can keep a permanent and chronological record of God's faithfulness by noting progress toward answered prayers and recording the dates of answers. This will, in turn, increase your faith in God's limitless love, power and resources. We've added pages to allow you to record impressions of your daily devotions or to journal your thoughts.

Sunday

Prayer Focus: *Pray for the nations and peoples of the world.*

Pray for all who are in authority—believers, nonbelievers, missions, the persecuted and those who suffer.

Pray for manpower, resources and opportunity to translate, produce and distribute the gospel among the unreached peoples of the world.

Pray for the penetration of the gospel into all areas of the world where there is not yet freedom to proclaim the gospel.

Meditate on His Attribute: Because GOD is holy . . . I will devote myself to Him in purity, worship and service.

> Who else among the gods is like you, O LORD—glorious in holiness like you—so awesome in splendor, performing such wonders? (Exod. 15:11).

Our God is holy. His character is perfect in every way. His moral excellence is the absolute standard of integrity and ethical purity. God's supreme holiness infinitely sets Him apart from His creation.

Rather than reflecting the opinions and attitudes of this broken world, you are to reflect the beauty of God's holiness. But in order to reflect God's holiness, you must first be made holy. And you can be made holy only by placing your faith in Jesus Christ.

As the holiness of God works into the fabric of your being, you will become sensitive to sin and self-centeredness, learning to abhor it as God does. As your life is transformed, you will project the light of His holiness into the darkness of this world.

God's holiness demands your devotion. Where is your heart? Holy living involves a daily decision to surrender to the lordship of Christ.

> But now you must be holy in everything you do, just as God—who chose you to be his children—is holy (1 Pet. 1:15).

My Sunday Thoughts

_____

_____

_____

_____

_____

_____

_____

_____

_____

_____

_____

_____

_____

_____

_____

_____

_____

Vonette Bright · www.regalbooks.com

Monday

Prayer Focus: Pray for the leaders of our country by name—that they might have protection, guidance, wisdom and awareness of God's presence in mind and heart and that they might practice integrity. Pray that:

- They might trust in God with all their heart and not lean on their own understanding; that they will acknowledge Him in all their ways (see Prov. 3:5-6).

- They will seek to have a conscience void of offense toward God and men (see Acts 24:16).

- God will place men and women of righteousness in positions of authority to lead the nations in righteousness (see Prov. 14:34; 16:12).

- Legislation in our country will be in line with principles from the Word of God.

- Christians will be aware of governmental issues, will support leaders in prayer and act rightly regarding issues concerning the moral and spiritual climate of our country.

Meditate on His Attribute: Because GOD is Sovereign . . . I will joyfully submit to His will.

Yours, O LORD, is the greatness, the power, the glory, the victory, and the majesty. Everything in the heavens and on earth is yours, O LORD, and this is your kingdom (1 Chron. 29:11).

Do you feel overwhelmed by circumstances? Be encouraged: Your loving God is still in control, and He is sovereignly directing your life. In fact, difficulties and suffering are tools in God's sovereign hands with which He shapes you into the image of Jesus. Nothing occurs without His divine permission.

God is the sovereign ruler of the universe. There is no higher authority. He is all-powerful, so no one can force Him to do anything against His will. He is present everywhere, so no one can hide from Him or escape His scrutiny. He is all-knowing, so there is nothing about which He is unaware.

God is actively directing His creation on a course that has been charted before the beginning of time. But within the context of His master plan, He gives each person the freedom to choose how he or she will participate. Will you choose to cooperate with Him?

God causes everything to work together for the good of those who love God and are called according to his purpose for them (Rom. 8:28).

My Monday Thoughts

Vonette Bright · www.regalbooks.com

Tuesday

Prayer Focus: Pray for the leaders of your state, county and city (see Ps. 127:1; Rom. 13:1-5). Pray that:

- God will give Christian leaders knowledge and discernment so they may be able to distinguish between right and wrong (see Phil. 1:9-10).

- God will expose unrighteousness in high places. Ask that He will grant repentance to unbelievers leading to a knowledge of the truth, and that those who are sensitive to His Spirit will remain in their positions of authority (see Prov. 10:9; Dan. 2:21; 2 Tim. 2:25).

Meditate on His Attribute: Because GOD is absolute truth . . . I will believe what He says and live accordingly.

[Jesus said] "I was born for that purpose. And I came to bring truth to the world. All who love the truth recognize that what I say is true" (John 18:37).

God wants us to know the truth. He gave us the Bible to help us understand the truth. He guides us into truth through the Holy Spirit.

God revealed truth to us in the person of Jesus, who said, "I am the way, the truth, and the life" (John 14:6). While many people claim to know the truth, only Jesus could honestly claim to *be* the truth.

God is the source of all truth because He is present everywhere, knows all things and totally understands what is real, right and true. Therefore, whatever He says is absolutely true.

God is our anchor in a society of relativism and falsehood. Do your actions demonstrate that you have bought into the lies of popular culture? Or are you consistently discovering truth in God's Word?

The truth will only be found by those who diligently and honestly seek it. Commit yourself daily to walk in the light of God's truth. God is truth.

Teach me your ways, O LORD, that I may live according to your truth! (Ps. 86:11).

My Tuesday Thoughts

_____

_____

_____

_____

_____

_____

_____

_____

_____

_____

_____

_____

_____

Vonette Bright · www.regalbooks.com

Vonette Bright · www.regalbooks.com

Wednesday

Prayer Focus: Pray for those undergoing persecution, imprisonment or privation. Pray for:

- All persons being persecuted for their commitment to Christ around the world (see Ps. 91:14-16)

- Prisoners of drugs, alcohol, immorality, obscenity, pornography, crime, prejudice, unbelief and despair (see Matt. 5:44-45; John 8:31-32,36; Rom. 6:19-23; 1 Cor. 10:13; 2 Cor. 3:17)

- Prisoners of poverty and hunger (see 1 Sam. 2:8; Job 5:15-16; Pss. 34:10; 50:14-15; Phil. 4:19)

Meditate on His Attribute: Because GOD is love . . . He is unconditionally committed to my wellbeing.

> This is real love. It is not that we loved God, but that he loved us and sent his Son as a sacrifice to take away our sins (1 John 4:10).

God's love is unconditional. It is not based on how good you are. He loves you because He is God and you are His creation.

God's love never fails. His love will not be terminated because of disappointment or a change of heart. He defines love and He demonstrates what true love looks like—Jesus gave His life on your behalf.

We, in turn, are to love God wholeheartedly. God has created us to find our greatest joy and fulfillment in loving Him.

God also enables us to be channels of His supernatural love. On our own, we are incapable of loving as we should, but God has an unending supply of love. It is for us to claim, to enjoy, and to share with others.

When we begin to love God, love our neighbors as ourselves and love our enemies, society will change for the better through the transforming power of God's love.

> Nothing in all creation will ever be able to separate us from the love of God that is revealed in Christ Jesus our Lord (Rom. 8:39).

My Wednesday Thoughts

_____
_____
_____
_____
_____
_____
_____
_____
_____
_____
_____
_____
_____
_____
_____

Vonette Bright · www.regalbooks.com

Thursday

Prayer Focus: Pray for the church and for church-related organizations, locally and worldwide. Pray for:

- Unity within the Body of Christ and for the evangelization of the world (see John 17:11; Acts 4:29,32; 1 Tim. 2:4)

- Pastors, deacons, elders, evangelists

- God's servants to walk in a manner worthy of the calling (see Eph. 4:1-3)

- Each messenger of God—that they may speak with boldness (see Eph. 6:19)

- God's men and women to be devoted to prayer (see Acts 1:14; 2:42)

- God's servants to cleanse themselves from all defilement of flesh and spirit, and live in the fear of God (see 2 Cor. 7:1)

- Good stewardship of resources and the proper commitment of all financial needs to God

- God's people to learn to engage in good deeds to meet pressing needs, that they may not be unfruitful (see Titus 3:14)

Meditate on His Attribute: Because GOD is all-powerful . . . He can help me with anything.

O Sovereign LORD! You have made the heavens and earth by your great power. Nothing is too hard for you! (Jer. 32:17).

Do you ever feel overwhelmed? Our all-powerful Creator who cares for us longs to exhibit His power in our lives.

No matter what you might be facing, God can help you. Nothing is too hard for Him. No need is too great for Him to meet. No problem is too complicated for Him to solve. No foe is too strong for Him to conquer. No prayer is too difficult for Him to answer.

God merely spoke and the universe sprang into being. But all the power contained in the entire universe is but a drop compared to God's unlimited power.

The Bible promises, "By His mighty power at work within us, he is able to accomplish infinitely more than we would ever dare to ask or hope" (Eph. 3:20).

If our hearts and motives are pure and we truly seek to do God's will, then there is nothing too difficult for us as we depend on His strength.

I can do everything with the help of Christ who gives me the strength I need (Phil. 4:13).

My Thursday Thoughts

Friday

Prayer Focus: Pray for greater Christian influence in mass media and cultural or social services. Pray:

- That publishers, producers, sponsors and performers will be awakened to God's principles and will recognize man's philosophy as empty deception
- For the public to crave righteousness to be portrayed in the entertainment field (see Matt. 5:6)
- That influential individuals in these fields will meet Christ and become ambassadors of reconciliation (see 2 Cor. 5:18-20)
- For God to impress upon your mind a list of personalities for whom He wishes you to pray

Meditate on His Attribute: Because GOD is righteous . . . I will live by His standards.

The LORD is righteous in everything he does; he is filled with kindness (Ps. 145:17).

We live in an age where the distinction between right and wrong is becoming increasingly blurred. Our culture has adopted the principle of situational ethics, which proposes that what is morally right varies from person to person and situation to situation. Yet God's standards do not change; they are timeless.

God's laws are a reflection of His own righteous nature. Only by receiving Jesus as our Savior and Lord are we made righteous, because we cannot keep God's perfect standard on our own.

However, God wants you to display His righteousness in your new life, but this is possible only as you consistently submit your will to the Holy Spirit and depend on Him to empower you.

As Christians, we must hold fast to the righteous standards set forth by the sovereign Ruler of the universe. God will hold every person accountable. Whose standards of right are you following?

"Abraham believed God, so God declared him to be righteous." He was even called "the friend of God" (Jas. 2:23).

My Friday Thoughts

_____

_____

_____

_____

_____

_____

_____

_____

_____

_____

_____

Vonette Bright · www.regalbooks.com

Saturday

Prayer Focus: Pray for fellow believers. Pray:

- For purification of our thoughts and deeds—that we may be fit instruments and channels of God's love (see Ps. 139:23-24)

- That Christians might encourage and stimulate one another to love and good deeds (see Heb. 10:24)

- For individual needs: spiritual, physical and material (see Phil. 4:6-7,19)

- That each may stand perfect and fully assured in all of the will of God (see Col. 4:12)

- For fellow believers' maturity and consistency in their personal Christian lives (see Eph. 3:14-20; Phil. 1:9-11)

Meditate on His Attribute: Because GOD is faithful . . . I will trust Him to always keep His promises.

> O LORD God Almighty! Where is there anyone as mighty as you, O LORD? Faithfulness is your very character (Ps. 89:8).

God is faithful to help you in your need. He will never fail you! He is reliable. He is trustworthy. Your holy and loving God is faithful!

God is faithful to forgive you even when you are unfaithful. Because you are still in a body of flesh, you have a tendency to be unfaithful. How encouraging it is to remember God's promise:

"If we are unfaithful, he remains faithful, for he cannot deny himself" (2 Tim. 2:13).

God is faithful to protect you from temptation. Remember, when you are tempted, do not focus on the attractiveness of the temptation, but on God's faithfulness to rescue you from that situation.

God is always faithful to keep His promises. He is ready and able to deliver all He has promised.

Faithfulness is at the heart of all that God is and does. His truthfulness, holiness, love, righteousness and other attributes ensure His faithfulness. He is incapable of being otherwise.

"God can be trusted to keep His promise" (Heb. 10:23).

My Saturday Thoughts

Vonette Bright · www.regalbooks.com

Appendices

Family Life Prayer Cards

Family Life Prayer for a Wife

Make me my husband's helpmate, companion, champion, friend and support. Help me to create a peaceful, restful, safe place for him to come home to. Teach me how to take care of myself and stay attractive to him. Grow me into a creative and confident woman who is rich in mind, soul and spirit. Make me the kind of woman he can be proud to say is his wife.

I lay all my expectations at Your cross. I release my husband from the burden of fulfilling me in areas where I should be looking to You. Help me to accept him the way he is and not try to change him . . . I leave any changing that needs to be done in Your hands, fully accepting that neither of us is perfect and never will be. Only You, Lord, are perfect and I look to You to perfect us.

Teach me how to pray for my husband and make my prayers a true language of love.

Lifting My Husband Through Prayer

LORD, thank You for my husband. I ask Your will for him in these things, according to Your Word.

Fill my husband with love for You, that he would love You "with all [his] heart and with all [his] soul and with all [his] mind" (Matthew 22:37-40).

Place his "delight . . . in the law of the LORD" (Psalm 1:2), and "open [his] eyes that [he] may behold wondrous things out of your law" (Psalm 119:18). Give him understanding (see Psalm 119:73).

Compel him to pray continually (see 1 Thessalonians 5:17) so that he'll live and walk by Your Spirit (see Galatians 5:25).

Empower him to "run with endurance the race that is set before [him]" and to focus on pleasing You (Hebrews 12:1-2).

Equip my husband with strength and wisdom to lead, that he would be "strong and very courageous," and that he may be successful where he goes (Joshua 1:7).

Supply him the time and ability to "manage his own household well" (1 Timothy 3:4).

Guide him in using wisely all the resources You've given us, keeping an eternal perspective about possessions (see Matthew 6:19-21; Luke 16:10-13).

May he share Your hatred of evil and experience Your protection (see Psalm 97:10).

Enable him to be "quick to hear, slow to speak, slow to anger" (James 1:19).

Help him to trust You "with all [his] heart" and not to "lean on [his] own understanding." Make his paths straight (see Proverbs 3:5).

Flood him with peace and faith (see Isaiah 26:3; John 14:1).

Increase his desire to teach and model godliness as a father, "that the next generation might know . . . and not forget the works of God" (Psalm 78:5-7).

Because You oppose the proud and give grace to the humble (see James 4:6), instill a genuine sense of humility in my husband's heart (see Isaiah 66:2).

Keep him sexually pure and honorable. "Blessed are the pure in heart, for they shall see God" (Matthew 5:8; see also 1 Corinthians 6:18-20).

Give him friendships with godly men (see Proverbs 27:17) that they would "stir up one another to love and good works" (Hebrews 10:24).

Let Your favor rest upon him and "establish the work of [his] hands" (Psalm 90:17).

And this is the confidence that we have toward You, Lord, that if we ask anything according to Your will, You hear us (see 1 John 5:14).

Lifting My Children Through Prayer

LORD, *thank You for my children. I ask Your will for them in these things, according to Your Word.*

Early in life, fill my children with love for You, that they would love You "with all [their] heart and with all [their] soul and with all [their] mind" (Matthew 22:37-40).

Train my children to love deeply, sincerely and sacrificially, seeing and loving others as You do (see 1 Peter 1:22; 1 John 3:16). Empower me to daily model Your love and compassion for them.

Give my children love for Your Word. Allow them to know and understand it, and to follow it wholeheartedly (see Psalm 1:1-3).

Fill them "with knowledge of [Your] will in all spiritual wisdom and understanding, so as to walk in a manner worthy of [You], fully pleasing to [You], bearing fruit in every good work and increasing in the knowledge of God" (Colossians 1:9-10; see also Psalm 90:17 and James 1:5).

Compel them to pray continually (see 1 Thessalonians 5:17), so that they will live and walk by Your Spirit (see Galatians 5:25). Help them to listen to You as Samuel did (see 1 Samuel 3:10).

Help me to train my children according to the unique way You've designed each one (see Proverbs 22:6; 1 Corinthians 12:4-7; Ephesians 2:10).

Enable me to commit them to Your loving care and control rather than worry about them (see Philippians 4:6; 1 Peter 5:7).

Give them godly friends (see Proverbs 27:17), that they would "stir up one another to love and good works" (Hebrews 10:24).

Cause them to be—and to find—a godly spouse (see Proverbs 31:10-12; Ephesians 5:25-28) or to glorify You in singleness (see 1 Corinthians 7:7-8). Keep them sexually pure and honorable (see 1 Corinthians 6:18-20).

Help them to be thankful and content (see 1 Thessalonians 5:18; 1 Timothy 6:6).

Be their shield in mind, heart and body (see Psalm 28:7). Guard them from the evil one (see 2 Thessalonians 3:3).

Grant me wisdom and strength to raise my children in the "discipline and instruction of the Lord" (Ephesians 6:4).

Let Your favor rest upon my children (see Psalm 90:17).

And this is the confidence that we have toward You, Lord, that if we ask anything according to Your will, You hear us (see 1 John 5:14).

Beginning Your Journey of Joy

These Four Principles Are Essential in Beginning a Journey of Joy

One—God loves you and created you to know Him personally.

God's Love
"God so loved the world that He gave His one and only Son, that whoever believes in Him shall not perish but have eternal life" (John 3:16).

God's Plan
"Now this is eternal life: that they may know you, the only true God, and Jesus Christ, whom you have sent" (John 17:3).

What prevents us from knowing God personally?

Two—People are sinful and separated from God, so we cannot know Him personally or experience His love.

People Are Sinful
"All have sinned and fall short of the glory of God" (Romans 3:23).

People were created to have fellowship with God; but, because of our own stubborn self-will, we chose to go our own independent way and fellowship with God was broken. This self-will, characterized by an attitude of active rebellion or passive indifference, is an evidence of what the Bible calls sin.

People Are Separated

"The wages of sin is death" [spiritual separation from God] (Romans 6:23).

This diagram illustrates that God is holy and people are sinful. A great gulf separates the two. The arrows illustrate that people are continually trying to reach God and establish a personal relationship with Him through our own efforts, such as a good life, philosophy, or religion—but we inevitably fail.

The third principle explains the only way to bridge this gulf . . .

Three—*Jesus Christ is God's only provision for our sin. Through Him alone we can know God personally and experience His love.*

He Died in Our Place

"God demonstrates His own love toward us, in that while we were yet sinners, Christ died for us" (Romans 5:8).

He Rose from the Dead

"Christ died for our sins . . . He was buried . . . He was raised on the third day according to the Scriptures . . . He appeared to Peter, then to the twelve. After that He appeared to more than five hundred . . ." (1 Corinthians 15:3-6).

He Is the Only Way to God

"Jesus said to him, 'I am the way, and the truth, and the life; no one comes to the Father but through Me'" (John 14:6).

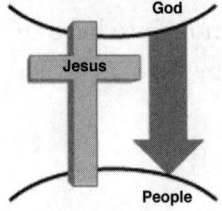

This diagram illustrates that God has bridged the gulf that separates us from Him by sending His Son, Jesus Christ, to die on the cross in our place to pay the penalty for our sins.

It is not enough just to know these three truths . . .

Four—We must individually receive Jesus Christ as Savior and Lord; then we can know God personally and experience His love.

We Must Receive Christ

"As many as received Him, to them He gave the right to become children of God, even to those who believe in His name" (John 1:12).

We Receive Christ Through Faith

"By grace you have been saved through faith; and that not of yourselves, it is the gift of God; not as a result of works that no one should boast" (Ephesians 2:8,9).

When We Receive Christ, We Experience a New Birth

(Read John 3:1-8.)

We Receive Christ by Personal Invitation

[Christ speaking] "Behold, I stand at the door and knock; if anyone hears My voice and opens the door, I will come in to him" (Revelation 3:20).

Receiving Christ involves turning to God from self (repentance) and trusting Christ to come into our lives to forgive us of our sins and to make us what He wants us to be. Just to agree intellectually that Jesus Christ is the Son of God and that He died on the cross for our sins is not enough. Nor is it enough to have an emotional experience. We receive Jesus Christ by faith, as an act of our will.

These two circles represent two kinds of lives:

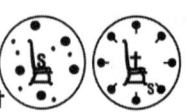

Self-Directed Life
S – Self is on the throne
† – Christ is outside the life
● – Interests are directed by self, often resulting in discord and frustration

Christ-Directed Life
† – Christ is in the life and on the throne
S – Self is yielding to Christ
● – Interests are directed by Christ, resulting in harmony with God's plan

Which circle best represents your life?
Which circle would you like to have represent your life?

The following explains how you can receive Christ:

You Can Receive Christ Right Now by Faith Through Prayer
(Prayer is talking with God)

God knows your heart and is not so concerned with your words as He is with the attitude of your heart. The following is a suggested prayer:

> *Lord Jesus, I want to know You personally. Thank You for dying on the cross for my sins. I open the door of my life and receive You as my Savior and Lord. Thank You for forgiving my sins and giving me eternal life. Take control of the throne of my life. Make me the kind of person You want me to be.*

Does this prayer express the desire of your heart?

If it does, I invite you to pray this prayer right now, and Christ will come into your life, as He promised.

How to Know That Christ Is in Your Life

Did you receive Christ into your life? According to His promise in Revelation 3:20, where is Christ right now in relation to you? Christ said that He would come into your life. Would He mislead you? On what authority do you know that God has answered your prayer? (The trustworthiness of God Himself and His Word.)

The Bible Promises Eternal Life to All Who Receive Christ

"The witness is this, that God has given us eternal life, and this life is in His Son. He who has the Son has the life; he who does not have the Son of God does not have the life. These things I have written to you who believe in the name of the Son of God, in order that you may know that you have eternal life" (1 John 5:11–13).

Thank God often that Christ is in your life and that He will never leave you (Hebrews 13:5). You can know on the basis of His promise that Christ lives in you and that you have eternal life from the very moment you invite Him in. He will not deceive you.

An important reminder . . .

Feelings Can Be Unreliable

You might have expectations about how you should feel after placing your trust in Christ. While feelings are important, they are unreliable indicators of your sincerity or the trustworthiness of God's promise. Our feelings change easily, but God's Word and His character remain constant. This illustration shows the relationship among *fact* (God and His Word), *faith* (our trust in God and His Word), and our *feelings*.

Fact: The chair is strong enough to support you.
Faith: You believe this chair will support you, so you sit in it.
Feeling: You may or may not feel comfortable in this chair, but it continues to support you.

The promise of God's Word, the Bible—not our feelings—is our authority. The Christian lives by faith (trust) in the trustworthiness of God Himself and His Word.

Now That You Have Entered Into a Personal Relationship With Christ

The moment you received Christ by faith, as an act of your will, many things happened, including the following:

1. Christ came into your life (Revelation 3:20; Colossians 1:27).
2. Your sins were forgiven (Colossians 1:14).
3. You became a child of God (John 1:12).
4. You received eternal life (John 5:24).

5. You began the great adventure for which God created you (John 10:10; 2 Corinthians 5:17; 1 Thessalonians 5:18).

Can you think of anything more wonderful that could happen to you than entering into a personal relationship with Jesus Christ? Would you like to thank God in prayer right now for what He has done for you? By thanking God, you demonstrate your faith.

To enjoy your new relationship with God...

Suggestions for Christian Growth
Spiritual growth results from trusting Jesus Christ. "The righteous man shall live by faith" (Galatians 3:11). A life of faith will enable you to trust God increasingly with every detail of your life, and to practice the following:

G   *Go* to God in prayer daily (John 15:7).

R   *Read* God's Word daily (Acts 17:11); begin with the Gospel of John.

O   *Obey* God moment by moment (John 14:21).

W   *Witness* for Christ by your life and words (Matthew 4:19; John 15:8).

T   *Trust* God for every detail of your life (1 Peter 5:7).

H   *Holy Spirit*—allow Him to control and empower your daily life and witness (Galatians 5:16,17; Acts 1:8; Ephesians 5:18).

Fellowship in a Good Church

God's Word admonishes us not to forsake "the assembling of ourselves together" (Hebrews 10:25). Several logs burn brightly together, but put one aside on the cold hearth and the fire goes out. So it is with your relationship with other Christians. If you do not belong to a church, do not wait to be invited. Take the initiative; call the pastor of a nearby church where Christ is honored and His Word is preached. Start this week, and make plans to attend regularly.

Adapted from *Would You Like to Know God Personally*, a version of the Four Spiritual Laws written by Bill Bright. © 2007 Bright Media Foundation and Campus Crusade for Christ, Inc., Orlando, Florida.

Satisfied?

Satisfaction: (n.) fulfillment of one's needs, longings, or desires

What words would you use to describe your current experience as a Christian?

Growing	Intimate	Exciting
Disappointing	Painful	Empty
Forgiven	Guilty	Duty
Struggling	So-so	Mediocre
Defeated	Frustrated	Dynamic
Up and down	Fulfilled	Vital
Discouraged	Stuck	Others?
	Joyful	

Do you desire more? Jesus said, "If anyone is thirsty, let him come to me and drink. Whoever believes in me, as the Scripture has said, streams of living water will flow from within him" (John 7:37,38).

What did Jesus mean? John, the biblical author, went on to explain, "By this he meant the Spirit, whom those who believed in him were later to receive. Up to that time the Spirit had not been given, since Jesus had not yet been glorified" (John 7:39).

Jesus promised that God's Holy Spirit would satisfy the thirst, or deepest longings, of all who believe in Jesus Christ. However, many Christians do not understand the Holy Spirit or how to experience Him in their daily lives.

The following principles will help you understand and enjoy God's Spirit.

The Divine Gift
Divine: (adj.) given by God

God has given us His Spirit so that we can experience intimacy with Him and enjoy all He has for us.

The Holy Spirit is the source of our deepest satisfaction.

The Holy Spirit is God's permanent presence with us.

> "Jesus said, 'I will ask the Father, and he will give you another Counselor to be with you forever—the Spirit of truth'" (John 14:16,17).

The Holy Spirit enables us to understand and experience all God has given us.

> We have not received the spirit of the world but the Spirit who is from God, that we may understand what God has freely given us (1 Corinthians 2:12).

The Holy Spirit enables us to experience many things:

- A genuine new spiritual life (John 3:1-8).
- The assurance of being a child of God (Romans 8:15,16).
- The infinite love of God (Romans 5:5; Ephesians 3:18,19).

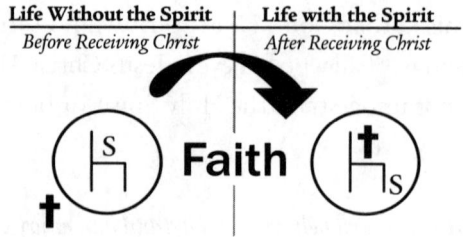

Vonette Bright · www.regalbooks.com

"The man without the Spirit does not accept the things that come from the Spirit of God, for they are foolishness to him, and he cannot understand them, because they are spiritually discerned" (1 Corinthians 2:14). "The spiritual man makes judgments about all things. . . . We have the mind of Christ" (1 Corinthians 2:15,16).

"But those who are controlled by the Holy Spirit think about things that please the Spirit" (Romans 8:5, *NLT*).

Why are many Christians not satisfied in their experience with God?

The Present Danger
Danger: (n.) a thing that may cause injury, loss, or pain

We cannot experience intimacy with God and enjoy all He has for us if we fail to depend on His Spirit.
People who trust in their own efforts and strength to live the Christian life will experience failure and frustration, as will those who live to please themselves rather than God.

We cannot live the Christian life in our own strength.

"Are you so foolish? After beginning with the Spirit, are you now trying to attain your goal by human effort?" (Galatians 3:3).

We cannot enjoy all God desires for us if we live by our self-centered desires.

"For the sinful nature desires what is contrary to the Spirit, and the Spirit what is contrary to the sinful nature.

They are in conflict with each other, so that you do not do what you want" (Galatians 5:17).

Three Kinds of Lifestyles

A Self-centered Life	A Christ-centered Life	A Self-Centered Life
Before Receiving Christ	*After Receiving Christ*	

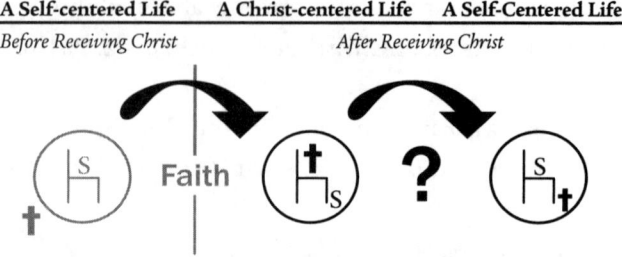

Faith   ?

"Brothers, I could not address you as spiritual, but as worldly—mere infants in Christ. I gave you milk, not solid food, for you were not yet ready for it. Indeed, you are still not ready. You are still worldly. For since there is jealousy and quarreling among you, are you not worldly? Are you not acting like mere men?" (1 Corinthians 3:1-3).

How can we develop a lifestyle of depending on the Spirit?

The Intimate Journey
Journey: (n.) any course from one experience to another

By walking in the Spirit we increasingly experience intimacy with God and enjoy all He has for us.
Walking in the Spirit moment by moment is a lifestyle. It is learning to depend upon the Holy Spirit for His abundant resources as a way of life.

As we walk in the Spirit, we have the ability to live a life pleasing to God.

"So I say, live by the Spirit, and you will not gratify the desires of the sinful nature. . . . Since we live by the Spirit, let us keep in step with the Spirit" (Galatians 5:16,25).

As we walk in the Spirit, we experience intimacy with God and all He has for us.

"But the fruit of the Spirit is love, joy, peace, patience, kindness, goodness, faithfulness, gentleness and self-control" (Galatians 5:22,23).

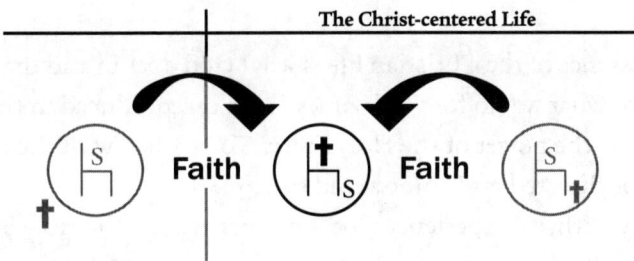

Faith (trust in God and His promises) is the only way a Christian can live by the Spirit.

Spiritual breathing is a powerful word picture which can help you experience moment-by-moment dependence upon the Spirit.

Exhale: Confess your sin the moment you become aware of it—agree with God concerning it and thank Him for His forgiveness, according to 1 John 1:9 and Hebrews 10:1-25. Confession requires repentance—a change in attitude and action.

Inhale: Surrender control of your life to Christ, and rely upon the Holy Spirit to fill you with His presence and power by faith, according to His command (Ephesians 5:18) and promise (1 John 5:14,15).

How does the Holy Spirit fill us with His power?

The Empowering Presence

Empower: (v.) to give ability to

We are filled with the Spirit by faith, enabling us to experience intimacy with God and enjoy all He has for us.

The essence of the Christian life is what God does in and through us, not what we do for God. Christ's life is reproduced in the believer by the power of the Holy Spirit. To be filled with the Spirit is to be directed and empowered by Him.

By faith, we experience God's power through the Holy Spirit.

"I pray that out of his glorious riches he may strengthen you with power through his Spirit in your inner being, so that Christ may dwell in your hearts through faith" (Ephesians 3:16,17).

Three important questions to ask yourself:

1. Am I ready now to surrender control of my life to our Lord Jesus Christ? (Romans 12:1,2).

2. Am I ready now to confess my sins? (1 John 1:9). Sin grieves God's Spirit (Ephesians 4:30). But God in His love has forgiven all of your sins—past, present, and future—because Christ has died for you.

3. Do I sincerely desire to be directed and empowered by the Holy Spirit? (John 7:37-39).

By faith claim the fullness of the Spirit according to His command and promise:

God COMMANDS us to be filled with the Spirit.

". . . Be filled with the Spirit" (Ephesians 5:18).

God PROMISES He will always answer when we pray according to His will.

"This is the confidence we have in approaching God: that if we ask anything according to his will, he hears us. And if we know that he hears us—whatever we ask—we know that we have what we asked of him" (1 John 5:14,15).

How to pray to be filled with the Holy Spirit . . .

The Turning Point

Turning point: time when a decisive change occurs

We are filled with the Holy Spirit by faith alone.

Sincere prayer is one way of expressing our faith. The following is a suggested prayer:

Dear Father, I need You. I acknowledge that I have sinned against You by directing my own life. I thank You that You have forgiven my sins through Christ's death on the cross for me. I now invite Christ to again take His place on the throne of my life. Fill me

with the Holy Spirit as You commanded me to be filled, and as You
promised in Your Word that You would do if I asked in faith. I pray
this in the name of Jesus. I now thank You for filling me with the
Holy Spirit and directing my life.

Does this prayer express the desire of your heart? If so, you can
pray right now and trust God to fill you with His Holy Spirit.

How to know that you are filled by the Holy Spirit:

- Did you ask God to fill you with the Holy Spirit?
- Do you know that you are now filled with the Holy Spirit?
- On what authority? (On the trustworthiness of God
  Himself and His Word: Hebrews 11:6; Romans 14:22,23.)

As you continue to depend on God's Spirit moment by moment you will experience and enjoy intimacy with God and all He
has for you—a truly rich and satisfying life.

An important reminder . . .

Do Not Depend on Feelings

The promise of God's Word, the Bible—not our feelings—is our authority. The Christian lives by faith (trust) in the trustworthiness
of God Himself and His Word. Flying in an airplane can illustrate
the relationship among fact (God and His Word), faith (our trust
in God and His Word), and feeling (the result of our faith and obedience) (John 14:21).

To be transported by an airplane, we must place our faith in the trustworthiness of the aircraft and the pilot who flies it. Our feelings of confidence or fear do not affect the ability of the airplane to transport us, though they do affect how much we enjoy the trip. In the same way, we as Christians do not depend on feelings or emotions, but we place our faith (trust) in the trustworthiness of God and the promises of His Word.

Now That You Are Filled with the Holy Spirit

Thank God that the Spirit will enable you:

- To glorify Christ with your life (John 16:14).
- To grow in your understanding of God and His Word (1 Corinthians 2:14,15).
- To live a life pleasing to God (Galatians 5:16-23).

Remember the promise of Jesus:

"But you will receive power when the Holy Spirit comes on you; and you will be my witnesses in Jerusalem, and in all Judea and Samaria, and to the ends of the earth" (Acts 1:8).

If you would like additional resources on the Holy Spirit, please go to **www.nlpdirect.com**.

Adapted from *Have You Made the Wonderful Discovery of the Spirit-filled Life?* Written by Bill Bright, © 1966, 1995 Campus Crusade for Christ International, Orlando, Florida.

Also Available from
Vonette Bright

In His Hands
Vonette Bright
ISBN 978.08307.54977
ISBN 08307.54970

The heavenly Father does not ask His children to live perfect Christian lives . . . and what a relief, as that is impossible even for the "giants of faith" who have led the Church throughout the centuries! Instead, our God asks us to place our hand in His and walk with Him through the adventure of life. This trust—the kind of trust that refuses to let go of God whether in good times or bad—is at the heart of a life of faith. Vonette Bright, co-founder with her husband, Bill Bright, of Campus Crusade for Christ, has walked with God for more than half a century. In this warm and personal book, she draws on her experiences to share what you can expect on your own faith adventures. You'll explore with Vonette how to take one step at a time with God by living through the power of the Holy Spirit, by serving others and by spreading the gospel, and find for yourself a walk with God—a life of faith—that sustains you, encourages you and gives you hope.